SECRETS
OF
SALT-FREE
COOKING

Jeanne Jones

101 PRODUCTIONS

Publisher Brete C. Harrison
VP and Director of Operations Linda Hauck
VP Marketing and Business Development John A. Morris
Associate Publisher James Connolly
Director of Production Steve Lux
Editors Barbara Feller-Roth, Susanne Fitzpatrick, and Annette Gooch
Proofreader Carolyn Chandler
Interior Designers Linda Hauck and Charlene Mouille
Production Assistant Dotti Hydue

Photography Keith Ovregaard
Food/Photographic Stylist Stephanie Greenleigh
Assistant Food Stylist Laura Jerrard

Printed and bound in Singapore.

Published by 101 Productions/Cole Group, Inc.
1330 N. Dutton Ave., Suite 103
P.O. Box 4089, Santa Rosa, CA 95402-4089
(800) 959-2717   (707) 526-2682
FAX (707) 526-2687

B   C   D   E   F   G   H
4   5   6   7   8   9   0

Library of Congress Catalog Card Number in progress.

ISBN 1-56426-504-8

Distributed to the book trade by Publishers Group West.

To my editor, Barbara Feller-Roth

With grateful thanks to
William Hansen, for technical advice and computer analysis
Taita Pearn, M.S., R.D., for technical research and consulting
Leni Reed, M.P.H., R.D., for nutritional consulting
Tracy DeMas, for recipe testing
Betty Wied, for recipe testing

Special thanks to
Mr. Mocha, Walnut Creek
Susan Eslick
Amy Nathan

Contents

Foreword, 7
Introduction, 9
The Low-Sodium Diet, 11
Dining Out, 13
Stocks and Soups, 15
Sauces, Gravies, and Condiments, 28
Salad Dressings, 43
Salads, 49
Vegetables, 57
Eggs, Egg Substitute, and Cheese, 75
Fish and Shellfish, 84
Poultry, 95
Meats, 105
Bread, Pancakes, Cereals, Etc., 118
Desserts, 138
Beverages, 158
Secret Suggestions and Important Facts, 164
Kitchen Vocabulary, 165
Sodium and Calorie Guide, 170
Equivalents, 175
U.S. Measure and Metric Measure Conversion Chart, 179
Bibliography, 180
Index, 182

People in the industrialized world consume five to thirty times as much salt (sodium chloride) as they need to maintain good health. Fortunately, in 70 to 80 percent of these people, the kidneys can handle this tremendous excess at least until age fifty or sixty, when tolerance for salt may be reduced. In this age group people need have no fear of eating too much salt unless their blood pressure begins to climb. The remaining 20 to 30 percent of the population will develop or have already developed high blood pressure because they ingest up to 30 times as much salt as their bodies need. (A doctor can determine salt consumption with a simple urinalysis.)

What evidence is there that salt has anything to do with high blood pressure? Consider the following points:

1. When one relatively unmixed ethnic group is compared with another with respect to the number of cases of high blood pressure, the higher the habitual salt intake, the higher the incidence of high blood pressure.

2. In any ethnic group where the habitual salt intake is less than 500 milligrams of sodium per day, the incidence of high blood pressure approaches zero.

3. Experiments with animals suggest that the ability to tolerate high-salt diets without developing high blood pressure may be determined genetically. For some species, salt even in very large amounts does not cause high blood pressure. For others, chronic ingestion of even moderate amounts of salt invariably causes high blood pressure.

4. For humans, a case in point may be African-Americans, whose ancestors may have become genetically intolerant, through evolution, of salt because of its scarcity in their environment. When in the eighteenth century these people were shipped as slaves to the high-salt culture of North America, high blood pressure

began to take its toll. Today, high blood pressure is much more severe and much more common among African-Americans than among any other cultural subgroup in America.

It follows, then, that African-Americans are part of the 20 to 30 percent of the population who are at risk of developing high blood pressure. Other high-risk groups include people with a family history of high blood pressure, and most particularly 95 percent of patients who develop even mild kidney failure. In these segments of the population, curtailing salt intake is of tremendous benefit. People acquire a taste for salt in infancy from being fed salty foods, but a low-salt diet, once learned, is relatively easy to follow. Unlike weight-reduction diets in which relapses are common, low-salt diets gain appeal as a person discovers—as in this excellent book—how to make low-salt dishes appetizing. The result is that people following a low-salt diet soon develop an aversion to salty foods.

For people at risk for developing high blood pressure, a low-salt diet is enormously beneficial. It can delay or avert altogether the onset of high blood pressure. In patients with very early or minimal kidney failure, a low-salt diet, by preventing high blood pressure, slows or even stops the progression of kidney damage. And for the millions of people who already have high blood pressure, reducing salt intake to very low levels will greatly reduce the amount of expensive antihypertensive medications they must take and the unwanted side effects that result from their use. In many cases these drugs can be discontinued completely if patients restrict salt intake to very low levels.

Belding H. Scribner, M.D.
Professor of Medicine
University of Washington School of Medicine

Simply leaving the salt out of recipes or not putting a saltshaker on the table, or both, is not the way to achieve a diet truly low in sodium. From birth we are so accustomed to having our food hyped with salt that we miss many delicate flavors. This book represents a new approach to seasoning foods and to reeducating the palate.

The medical profession recognizes that high blood pressure is more easily controlled if salt intake is moderately restricted. Vital organs such as the heart, kidneys, and liver are more likely to function properly on a low-sodium diet. Even health-care professionals who feel that the dangers of too much salt are overrated admit that most of us consume a great deal more salt than our bodies require. Healthy, active people need only about one teaspoon of salt, or approximately 2,000 milligrams of sodium, for every 1,000 calories of food consumed.

Unlike other restricted diets, which are based on portion control and the omission of certain foods, a low-sodium diet requires special recipes and ingredients. Even tap water in some areas is so high in sodium that distilled water is recommended for both drinking and cooking.

The major challenge in developing recipes for a low-sodium diet versus other modified diets is that salt is a basic taste for which there is no substitute. Taste buds recognize only four basic tastes: sweet, salt, sour, and bitter. In recipes for a low-sodium diet, it is necessary to fool the taste buds and make up for the lack of flavor-enhancing salt by stimulating one of the other basic tastes. All other "tastes" are actually smells. If you don't believe this, hold your nose the next time you are eating a favorite food and you will find that you do not taste it. By offering your palate a wide range of flavors, salt-free cooking will add a new dimension and importance to your sense of smell.

As anyone who has read my other books knows, I love to cook. I have become so fascinated with the concept of salt-free cooking that I am having fun developing new recipes and modifying the classics. In this book I include low-sodium recipes for basic items such as crackers, English muffins, sauces, salad dressings, and mayonnaise that are difficult or impossible to find commercially. I always specify low-sodium

sodium mayonnaise because regular commercial mayonnaise is very high in sodium. I suggest that you use my recipe for Unsalted Mayonnaise (see page 37) because I think you will like it better than any you can buy commercially. In addition, in my recipes I specifically call for corn oil margarine. Pure corn oil margarine is better for your health than some of the other mixed-oil margarines; it also has a better flavor when heated. Use monounsaturated or polyunsaturated oils for cooking. I always specify extra virgin olive oil or corn oil because I prefer their taste and texture.

To my delight, my friends seem to enjoy the meals I serve them more than ever since I began working on this book. They experience a whole range of delicate flavors that were buried before under too much added salt and other high-sodium ingredients. I think this book will open new horizons in the preparation and enjoyment of food for anyone on a sodium-restricted diet.

Because I love to entertain, a primary objective in writing *Secrets of Salt-Free Cooking* has been to provide you with recipes so delicious and unusual that you will be able to serve your friends exactly the same foods allowed on your diet program. You can have imaginative and elegant dinners and be rewarded by the many compliments of guests.

For dining in and out, this book may even inspire a French approach to healthier recipe modification—*la cuisine sans sel.*

Jeanne Jones

Before discussing the modifications necessary for a sodium-restricted diet, I want to explain what sodium is, where it comes from, and why it should be limited.

Sodium is a soft, waxy, silver-white element, the chemical symbol for which is *Na*. It occurs in nature combined with chlorine (chemical symbol *Cl*) to form sodium chloride (*NaCl*)—ordinary table salt, the kind used in saltshakers. Sodium makes up 40 percent by weight of table salt. There are 2,208 milligrams (2.2 grams) of sodium in one teaspoon of salt. Sodium is found in varying amounts in all foods of plant and animal origin, and even in water (unless the water has been distilled). The amount of sodium present in many foods can be found in the list on pages 170 to 174.

Sodium is necessary in the right amount for everyday good health. One of its major functions in the body is working with chlorine to regulate the pH of body fluids (*pH* is a value used to express relative acidity and alkalinity). In a properly functioning body, if the body fluids are too acidic, the kidneys excrete chlorine; if the body fluids are too alkaline, the kidneys excrete sodium. Sodium also regulates muscle contractions and affects nerve irritability.

Most people consume a great deal more sodium than is needed for proper bodily function. The excess is excreted by the kidneys. When the body is unable to rid itself of the extra sodium because of diseases of the heart, circulatory system, or kidneys, sodium accumulates. Since fluid accumulates along with the sodium, the result is fluid retention, which causes edema, a swelling of the tissues. Edema is dangerous because it makes the heart work harder and may cause a rise in blood pressure. When this condition occurs, restricting sodium intake may be necessary.

If you have high blood pressure or impaired function of any vital organ, your doctor may prescribe a low-sodium diet. The most frequently prescribed low-sodium diet is for 2,000 milligrams of sodium per day; however, in some cases the prescription is 500 milligrams or less of sodium per day. A diet restriction this low is extremely difficult to follow and requires constant monitoring of the foods consumed.

Here are some simple, basic measures you can take to reduce sodium consumption. In general, fruits have the lowest sodium content, whereas vegetables vary widely. Some vegetables that are very low in calories are high in sodium, so if you are counting calories as well as watching sodium intake, choose your vegetables with care (see Sodium and Calorie Guide starting on page 170) and use fresh vegetables if possible. Frozen or canned vegetables may have added salt; always read the labels.

The sodium content of local water supplies varies greatly from one area to another; check with your local water district. If there are more than 30 milligrams of sodium per quart, it is advisable to use distilled water for both drinking and cooking. Home water softeners add a great deal of sodium to the water; they may be fine for washing laundry or shampooing hair, but softened water should not be used for either drinking or cooking. Many nonprescription laxatives, cold remedies, tranquilizers, and headache medications are high in sodium, so check with your doctor before using them.

Still, my rule in writing this book about low-sodium diets has been "never say 'never'" to any ingredient. Obviously, you should avoid table salt and foods cured or processed with salt, such as ham, corned beef, pickles, and sauerkraut, to name a few. By carefully calculating the milligrams of sodium present in foods, however, you can occasionally have foods considered taboo in most sodium-restricted diets. If you are particularly fond of celery, artichokes, Parmesan cheese, Worcestershire sauce, or even clams, normally forbidden, you may use them sparingly, carefully calculating the total number of milligrams of sodium in order not to exceed your doctor's prescribed limitation. For this reason you will occasionally find ingredients in recipes in this book that you will not find in other low-sodium cookbooks.

Labels on low-sodium food products show the number of milligrams of sodium per serving, and the serving size. Be aware that some foods in the diet section of the market are for sugar-restricted diets only. It is important to read the labels carefully for sodium content. The more you learn about the nutritional content of foods and about low-sodium cooking in general, the more fun you will have cooking, eating, and entertaining—and the more you will be able to use your imagination in both developing new recipes and modifying old ones.

Coping with sodium restriction while dining out is a challenge that can be met optimistically. With the following tips you can deal effectively with a sodium-restricted diet while continuing to enjoy restaurant dining. The emphasis is on taking responsibility for what you eat, whether you are in a restaurant or in a friend's home. Waiters may be uninformed about the sodium content of foods, and friends may have the attitude that "a little won't hurt."

Before going to a restaurant, call and check to see if they have separate cruets of vinegar and oil, and unsalted butter or margarine. If they don't, you can bring low-sodium salad dressing with you (see pages 43 to 48), along with unsalted butter or margarine, including a cube to give to the kitchen in case you want to order your entrée sautéed. You can also bring unsalted crackers (see page 129) or melba toast, and even your own croutons (see page 119). When you arrive at the restaurant, inform your waiter that you can't have salt on anything. Your salad can have lettuce and fresh vegetables, but no canned or cooked vegetables, and no seafood or cooked dried beans. For your entrée, ask to have meat, fish, or poultry broiled with no salt or other seasoning, making sure it has not been marinated. If you order chicken, make sure it has not been precooked. Some restaurants precook the chicken with salt and then place it under the broiler to brown when ordered. Avoid soup, since it is almost always salted, and pasta, since it is usually cooked in salted water. Ask for an unopened baked potato. Before ordering rice, ask if it can be steamed or cooked without salt. (Avoid rice pilaf; it is almost always cooked with salt.) Ask if a vegetable can be steamed or boiled without salt in the water, and with no butter or margarine or seasoning added. Limit dessert to fresh, frozen, or canned fruit. Then, politely but firmly insist that the waiter inform the cook of your sodium restriction by writing "no salt on anything!" on your order.

If you enjoy dining out, select several restaurants where you know your instructions will be followed without making you feel as though you are imposing. (Avoid ethnic restaurants such as Chinese, Japanese,

Mexican, and Indian, since sodium restrictions are almost impossible to accommodate in these cuisines. Also, fast-food restaurants cannot usually make changes in their menus.) It may take a while to acquaint yourself with suitable restaurants, but after you have returned a few times they will remember you, and dining out will be hassle free.

When you dine in homes of friends, explain your sodium restriction. If your host or hostess offers to cook your portion of the menu without salt, make sure he or she understands how to do it, and offer to bring your own butter or margarine, salad dressing, and bread. Or offer to bring your own food. If you ask what will be served to other guests, you can bring a dinner as close to that as possible.

Airlines can accommodate many special diet restrictions. When making your reservation, request a low-sodium meal; then, when you arrive at the airport, make sure to ask if your food is on the plane. Carrying your own cheese and crackers is a good idea, so when salted peanuts are passed out, you have your own snack.

STOCKS AND SOUPS

Preparing your own stocks is important not only to control sodium content but also to improve flavor. Although commercially prepared low-sodium stocks, bouillons, and consommés are available, they are difficult to find and are often tasteless. Soups and sauces made with your own stocks will be more delicious and far less expensive than those made with commercial preparations. If your stocks seem weak in flavor, boil them down to evaporate more of the liquid and to concentrate the strength. I do this routinely because strong flavor is essential in low-sodium cooking.

This chapter contains recipes for easy-to-make stocks and for a variety of soups that are both flavorful and low in sodium, such as Baked French Onion Soup (see page 24), served steaming hot directly from the oven, and Spicy Gazpacho (see page 22), served very cold on a bed of ice. Soups can be served as a light first course with practically no calories—help yourself to Stracciatella alla Romana (see page 25)—or a hearty combination of ingredients suitable for an entrée, such as Sopa de Albondigas (see page 27). Soups are a versatile part of the menu, so enjoy!

Unsalted Beef Stock

Each serving contains negligible calories, cholesterol, fat, and sodium

4 pounds beef or veal bones
3 large unpeeled onions,
   quartered
2 carrots, scraped and sliced
6 cloves unpeeled garlic, halved
4 sprigs parsley
2 whole cloves
1 teaspoon celery seed
1 teaspoon each dried thyme
   and dried marjoram, crushed
2 bay leaves
12 black peppercorns
1 can (12 oz) unsalted tomato
   juice
1/4 cup white vinegar
Defatted beef drippings (see page
   29), optional
Distilled water, to cover

Browning the bones and vegetables prior to making beef stock will give it a rich, dark color and make appetizing-looking sauces and gravies. For added flavor without added calories or sodium, sauté your favorite vegetables in stock instead of fat.

Note that stock must be simmered 5 to 10 hours and chilled overnight before using.

Preheat oven to 400° F. In a roasting pan brown bones for 30 minutes. Add onions, carrots, and garlic; brown together until they are a rich, deep brown color (about 30 minutes more), turning frequently to brown evenly.

Place browned bones and vegetables in a large stockpot; add parsley, cloves, celery seed, thyme, marjoram, bay leaves, peppercorns, tomato juice, vinegar, and beef drippings (if used). Add distilled water to cover by 1 inch, and bring mixture slowly to a boil over medium heat. Simmer slowly for 5 minutes, removing any foam that forms on surface. Reduce heat to low and cover, leaving lid ajar; simmer slowly for at least 5 hours. (Ten hours is even better if you will be around to turn off the heat.)

Remove from heat and allow to stand until cool enough to handle. Remove and discard bones and vegetables. Strain stock and allow to cool to room temperature. Refrigerate, uncovered, overnight or until fat has congealed on top. Remove and discard fat; freeze stock that will not be used within 2 days.

Makes about 10 cups, ten 1-cup servings

Unsalted Chicken Stock

Each serving contains negligible calories, cholesterol, fat, and sodium

3 pounds chicken parts, such as
  wings and backs
1 whole stewing chicken
  (optional)
2 carrots, scraped and sliced
3 unpeeled onions, quartered
5 cloves unpeeled garlic, halved
2 sprigs parsley
2 bay leaves
1 teaspoon dried basil, crushed
12 peppercorns
1/4 cup white vinegar
Distilled water, to cover

Cooking a stewing chicken in homemade stock is helpful in two ways: It adds flavor to the stock, and it produces a beautifully seasoned chicken to serve for dinner or to use in preparing many other dishes, such as soups and sandwiches.

Note that this stock must simmer 6 to 7 hours and chill overnight, so allow for adequate preparation time.

Place all ingredients except distilled water in a large stockpot. Add distilled water to cover by 1 inch. Bring slowly to a boil over medium heat. Reduce heat to low and cover, leaving lid ajar; simmer very slowly for 6 to 7 hours. If using the whole chicken, remove it after 3 hours and continue to simmer stock for another 3 to 4 hours.

Remove stock from heat and allow to stand until cool enough to handle. Remove and discard chicken parts and vegetables. Strain stock and allow to cool to room temperature. Refrigerate stock, uncovered, overnight or until fat has congealed on top.

Remove and discard fat: freeze stock that will not be used within 2 days.

Makes about 10 cups, ten 1-cup servings

Unsalted Turkey Stock

Substitute 1 turkey carcass for the chicken and use herbs and spices of your choice.

Unsalted Fish Stock

Each serving contains negligible calories, cholesterol, fat, and sodium

2 pounds fish heads, bones, and
   trimmings
2 1/2 quarts distilled water
3 unpeeled onions, quartered
6 sprigs parsley
1 carrot, scraped and sliced
1 teaspoon dried marjoram,
   crushed
12 peppercorns
1/4 cup freshly squeezed lemon
   juice

Poaching fish and seafood in fish stock rather than water greatly improves their taste. Fish stock is also a valuable ingredient in most seafood sauces.

Place all ingredients in a large saucepan or stockpot and bring to a boil over medium heat. Reduce heat to low and simmer, uncovered, for 45 minutes.

Line a colander or strainer with damp cheesecloth and strain stock through it. Let stock cool to room temperature, then refrigerate. Freeze stock that will not be used within 2 days.

Makes about 8 cups, eight 1-cup servings

Unsalted Court Bouillon

Each serving contains negligible calories, cholesterol, fat, and sodium

1 1/2 quarts distilled water
2 cups dry white wine
1 unpeeled lemon, sliced
1 carrot, scraped and sliced
1 unpeeled onion, sliced
2 cloves unpeeled garlic, halved
2 bay leaves
1/2 teaspoon celery seed
1/4 teaspoon peppercorns
2 tablespoons freshly squeezed
   lemon juice

This court bouillon can be made ahead, and it can be used many times; just strain it after each use and freeze the remainder. Although fish stock is preferable for poaching fish, this court bouillon is easier to make and is completely satisfactory. Be careful not to overcook the seafood or it will become tough.

In a large saucepan or stockpot, combine all ingredients and bring to a boil over medium heat. Reduce heat to low and simmer, uncovered, for 45 minutes.

Strain mixture; discard solids and use liquid for cooking shrimp, crab, or lobster or for poaching fish.

Makes about 8 cups, eight 1-cup servings

Unsalted Vegetable Stock

Each serving contains negligible calories, cholesterol, fat, and sodium

1 pound cabbage, shredded
2 pounds onions, peeled and
  chopped
1 pound carrots, scraped and
  chopped
2 pounds celery stalks, chopped
$^1/_4$ pound parsley, chopped
2 bay leaves
2 teaspoons dried marjoram,
  crushed
1 gallon distilled water

Vegetable stock is an essential ingredient in a vegetarian kitchen. You can make vegetable stock from almost any combination of vegetables as long as you eliminate ingredients that might add bitterness, such as carrot peelings and celery leaves. Try my recipe and then experiment with your favorite vegetables. Use your imagination and leftover vegetables to create a variety of stocks in which to poach, steam, or sauté your favorite foods. Freeze some stock in ice cube trays to use in sautéing. Two ice cubes equal $^1/_4$ cup liquid.

In a large stockpot combine all ingredients and bring to a boil over medium heat. Reduce heat to low and cover, leaving lid ajar; simmer for 1 hour.

Strain stock; discard vegetables or purée them as a side dish. Refrigerate stock in a tightly covered container, or store in the freezer in the size containers you most often use.

Makes about 12 cups, twelve 1-cup servings

Unsalted Beef Bouillon

Each serving contains negligible calories, cholesterol, fat, and sodium

1 part Unsalted Beef Stock
  (see page 16)
1 part distilled water

Bouillon is simply weak stock. It is fabulous for cooking vegetables because it contributes so much flavor without adding much sodium or many calories.

Combine stock and water in a pan and bring to a boil over medium heat. Reduce heat to low and simmer for at least 15 minutes before using.

> ### Unsalted Chicken Bouillon
> Substitute 1 part Unsalted Chicken Stock (see page 17) for beef stock.

Unsalted Chicken Consommé

Each serving contains negligible calories, cholesterol, fat, and sodium

2 egg whites
4 cups cold Unsalted Chicken Stock (see page 17)
3 bay leaves
2 sprigs parsley
1 cup chopped green onion tops
Ground white pepper, to taste

Consommés are clarified stocks or bouillons. Whether you are serving consommé hot or cold, it should be beautifully clear. Egg whites are used to clarify the consommé in this recipe.

In a small bowl beat egg whites with a wire whisk until they are slightly foamy, then add 1 cup of the stock and beat together lightly.

Place remaining stock in a very clean saucepan with remaining ingredients. Bring to a boil over medium heat, then remove from heat.

Slowly pour egg-white mixture into hot stock, stirring with wire whisk. Place saucepan over very low heat and stir gently until mixture starts to simmer. Move pan halfway off the burner so the mixture is barely simmering; turn pan every few minutes to heat mixture evenly. Simmer for 40 minutes.

Line a colander or strainer with 2 or 3 layers of damp cheesecloth. Strain mixture, allowing it to drain undisturbed until it has all seeped through. Refrigerate consommé in a tightly covered container until ready to use.

Makes 3 cups, three 1-cup servings

Unsalted Beef Consommé

Substitute cold Unsalted Beef Stock (see page 16) for the chicken stock; 2 teaspoons dried chervil, crushed, for the bay leaves; and freshly ground black pepper for the white pepper. Proceed exactly as for Unsalted Chicken Consommé

Unsalted Sherried Consommé

Prepare Unsalted Chicken Consommé as directed. Just before serving, add 2 tablespoons dry sherry and stir well.

Unsalted Madrilene

Each serving contains 48 calories, no cholesterol, no fat, and 10 mg sodium

2 large ripe tomatoes, sliced
  (2 cups)
2 leeks, white part only,
  chopped (1 cup)
2 onions, peeled and sliced
  (4 cups)
1 carrot, scraped and sliced
  ($^1/_2$ cup)
2 tablespoons freshly squeezed
  lemon juice
$^1/_4$ teaspoon peppercorns
2 quarts Unsalted Chicken
  Stock (see page 17)
3 bay leaves
2 envelopes unflavored
  gelatin softened in $^1/_4$ cup
  cold water
Freshly ground black pepper,
  to taste

This is the easiest method of making a tomato-flavored consommé that I have ever come across. You don't have to strain it because all the sediment sinks to the bottom and can be removed easily after the madrilene has jelled.

In a large stockpot over medium heat, combine tomatoes, leeks, onions, carrot, lemon juice, peppercorns, stock, and bay leaves; bring to a boil. Reduce heat to low and cover, leaving lid ajar about 1 inch; simmer for 2 hours.

Add gelatin mixture to hot stock and stir until gelatin is completely dissolved. Let cool slightly, then strain through a fine strainer. Season with pepper.

Let madrilene cool to room temperature, then pour into a 1$^1/_2$-quart mold and refrigerate. When madrilene is completely jelled, unmold by loosening the edges with the tip of a sharp knife, then dipping the mold up to the rim in hot water for a few seconds, and inverting onto a plate. Discard the part containing sediment. Dice the clear part and serve cold in sherbet glasses or glass cups.

Makes about 6 cups, twelve $^1/_2$-cup servings

Cold Blueberry Soup

Each serving contains 98 calories, no cholesterol, negligible fat, and 11 mg sodium

3 cups fresh or unsweetened
   frozen blueberries
1 cup unsweetened pineapple
   juice
1 teaspoon freshly squeezed
   lemon juice
1/2 teaspoon vanilla extract
4 teaspoons nonfat plain yogurt

Blueberry soup makes an unusual and delicious first course for brunch. Serve it with Lettuce Bread (see page 125) and follow it with your choice of omelet (see pages 78 and 79). I serve the soup in bowls set on individual beds of ice and garnish each serving with a sprig of fresh mint.

In a blender place 2 cups of the blueberries, pineapple juice, lemon juice, and vanilla; blend until smooth.

Divide mixture among 4 chilled bowls, preferably set on individual beds of ice to keep the soup very cold. (The soup also looks elegant served this way.) Stir 1/4 cup of the remaining blueberries into each bowl and garnish each serving with 1 teaspoon yogurt.

Makes 3 cups, four 3/4-cup servings

Spicy Gazpacho

Each serving contains 44 calories, no cholesterol, negligible fat, and 88 mg sodium

2 cans (16 oz each) unsalted
   stewed tomatoes, undrained
1 medium onion, peeled and
   chopped (1 1/2 cups)
1 small green bell pepper,
   seeded and chopped (3/4 cup)
1 small cucumber, peeled and
   chopped (3/4 cup)
2 cloves garlic, chopped
1/2 teaspoon onion powder
1/4 teaspoon hot-pepper sauce
1/4 teaspoon freshly ground
   black pepper
1 cup chopped chives or green
   onion tops
2 lemons, quartered

You can serve this cold Mexican soup instead of a salad. I serve it with Toasted Tortilla Triangles (see page 122) as a first course before Pisces Mexicana (see page 87). Sometimes I add diced leftover cooked fish, chicken, or turkey to the gazpacho and serve it as a luncheon entrée.

Into a blender pour entire contents of 1 can of tomatoes and only juice from the second can. Dice tomatoes from the second can and set aside.

Add onion, bell pepper, cucumber, garlic, onion powder, hot-pepper sauce, and ground pepper; blend until puréed. Pour mixture into a large bowl, add diced tomatoes, and mix well. Chill well..

To serve, divide among 8 bowls and garnish each serving with 2 tablespoons chives and a lemon wedge.

Makes 5 1/3 cups, eight 2/3-cup servings

Hearty Lentil Soup

Each serving contains 249 calories, no cholesterol, 2 g fat, and 25 mg sodium

1 tablespoon unsalted corn oil
  margarine
1 medium onion, peeled and
  sliced (2 cups)
1 small green bell pepper, seeded
  and chopped ($^3/_4$ cup)
2 cloves garlic, minced
2 $^1/_2$ quarts (10 cups) Unsalted
  Beef Stock (see page 16)
2 bay leaves
1 teaspoon dried thyme, crushed
$^1/_4$ teaspoon freshly ground black
  pepper
1 tablespoon smoke flavoring
1 pound (2 $^1/_2$ cups) dried
  lentils, soaked in water to
  cover overnight and drained

There is not better soup to serve on a cold winter day. I also like to serve it as a summer appetizer, chilled and topped with a dollop of light sour cream and a sprig of thyme.

In a heavy skilled over medium heat, melt margarine. Add onion, bell pepper, and garlic; cook until vegetables are tender and lightly browned (about 10 minutes).

In a large saucepan over medium heat, blend stock, browned vegetables, bay leaves, thyme, ground pepper, and smoke flavoring; mix well. Add lentils and bring to a boil. Reduce heat; cover, leaving lid ajar, and simmer for 1$^1/_2$ hours. Serve hot.

Makes about 11 cups, eight 1$^1/_3$-cup servings

Baked French Onion Soup

Each serving contains 346 calories, 20 mg cholesterol, 15 g fat, and 25 mg sodium

8 very thin slices Low-Sodium
  French Bread (see page 120)
2 tablespoons unsalted corn oil
  margarine
2 medium onions, peeled and
  sliced vertically very thinly (4
  cups)
1/2 cup dry white wine
1/2 teaspoon freshly ground black
  pepper
Dash cayenne pepper
4 cups Unsalted Beef Stock (see
  page 16), boiling
1 cup grated low-sodium Swiss
  cheese

If you like French onion soup but almost always find restaurant versions too salty, you are going to love this recipe. When slicing the French bread, figure that two slices together should be no thicker than one typical slice.

Preheat oven to 300° F. On a baking sheet arrange bread slices so they do not touch, and place in oven until they are dry (about 5 minutes). Remove from oven and set aside; increase heat to 325° F.

In a large saucepan over medium heat, melt margarine. Add onions, cover, and over very low heat cook until onions are soft. Remove the lid, increase heat to high, and cook onions until they are nicely browned, stirring constantly so they do not burn.

Reduce heat to low; add wine and continue cooking until wine is almost completely absorbed. Add black pepper and cayenne and mix well. Add stock, mix well, and simmer for 5 minutes.

Divide soup among 4 ovenproof bowls and place 2 slices reserved bread on top of each. Allow to stand until bread is completely saturated with soup, then sprinkle 1/4 cup cheese over each serving. Bake, uncovered, until cheese is lightly browned (30 to 40 minutes). Serve hot.

Makes 4 cups, four 1-cup servings

Sherried Pea Soup
Each serving contains 125 calories, 1 mg cholesterol, 1 g fat, and 47 mg sodium

2 cups shelled peas
1 cup Unsalted Chicken Stock
  (see page 17)
1/8 teaspoon ground white
  pepper
1 cup nonfat milk
1/4 cup dry sherry
1/2 teaspoon freshly grated
  lemon zest, for garnish

This soup may be served hot, although I prefer it cold served on a bed of ice. Allow about 2 pounds of unshelled peas for the required 2 cups of shelled peas.

In a medium saucepan over medium heat, place peas, stock, and pepper. Bring to a boil, cover, and cook until peas are just tender (about 5 minutes). Remove from heat and let cool slightly.

In a blender place pea mixture, milk, and sherry; blend until smooth.

To serve hot, return mixture to saucepan and cook over medium heat until hot. To serve cold, transfer soup to a container, cover, and chill. Serve soup in chilled bowls set on ice. Sprinkle hot or cold soup with a pinch of grated lemon zest.

Makes 2 1/3 cups, four 1/3-cup servings

Stracciatella Alla Romana
Each serving contains 42 calories, 2 mg cholesterol, 1 g fat, and 65 mg sodium

4 cups Unsalted Chicken Stock
  (see page 17)
3 egg whites
1/8 teaspoon ground nutmeg
1 tablespoon freshly grated
  Romano cheese
2 tablespoons minced parsley

This famous Roman soup, with freshly grated Romano cheese and a hint of nutmeg, has always seemed to me like an Italian version of Chinese egg-drop soup, only better.

In a large saucepan over medium heat, bring stock to a boil.

In a small bowl beat together egg whites, nutmeg, and cheese; add parsley. Pour mixture into boiling stock, stirring continuously until egg whites are cooked (about 1 minute). Immediately ladle soup into 4 bowls and serve.

Makes 5 cups, four 1 1/4-cup servings

Minestrone

Each serving contains 199 calories, 15 mg cholesterol, 5 g fat, and 98 mg sodium

2 tablespoons extra virgin
  olive oil
3 cloves garlic, minced
1/2 pound lean pork, cut into
  1/2-inch cubes
1 medium onion, peeled and
  finely chopped (1 1/2 cups)
2 small zucchini, thinly sliced
  (3 cups)
1 leek, white part only, finely
  chopped (1/2 cup)
1/4 teaspoon freshly ground
  black pepper
1 teaspoon each dried oregano
  and dried basil, crushed
2 1/2 quarts (10 cups) Unsalted
  Beef Stock (see page 16)
1 cup dried kidney beans,
  soaked overnight in water to
  cover, rinsed, and drained
1 small head cabbage,
  shredded (8 cups)
6 large leaves romaine lettuce,
  cut into strips (3 cups)
1/2 cup finely chopped parsley
1 cup dry red wine
1/2 cup small elbow macaroni
1 can (14 1/2 oz) unsalted
  stewed tomatoes, undrained
2 tablespoons freshly squeezed
  lemon juice
1/4 cup freshly grated
  Parmesan cheese

With a tossed salad and warm crusty bread, this satisfying soup makes a filling winter meal. Because Parmesan cheese is high in sodium, very little is called for in this recipe. For maximum flavor, therefore, it is important to buy a high-quality Parmesan and grate it just before serving the soup.

In a large, heavy skillet over medium heat, warm oil. Add garlic and sauté until tender. Add pork and sauté until cooked and browned. Add onion, zucchini, leek, pepper, oregano, and basil. Cover and cook for 10 minutes.

In a large saucepan over medium heat, bring stock to a boil. Add pork mixture and beans and mix well. Add cabbage, lettuce, parsley, and wine; cook until beans are tender (about 1 1/2 hours).

Add macaroni and tomatoes in their juice; cook another 15 minutes. Just before serving, add lemon juice and mix well. Sprinkle 1 teaspoon cheese over each serving.

Makes 15 cups, twelve 1 1/4-cup servings

Sopa De Albondigas

Each serving contains 140 calories, 32 mg cholesterol, 3 g fat, and 77 mg sodium

1 medium onion, peeled and diced (1½ cups)
1 clove garlic, minced
½ teaspoon ground cumin
1 can (8 oz) low-sodium tomato sauce
3 cups Unsalted Beef Stock (see page 16)
Mexican Meatballs uncooked (see page 111)
1 tablespoon freshly squeezed lemon juice
Dash hot-pepper sauce (optional)

This Mexican meatball soup makes a wonderful luncheon entrée served with Toasted Tortilla Triangles (see page 122) and a tossed green salad. For dessert serve a colorful assortment of fresh fruit. Although the nutritional analysis for the soup includes the meatballs, figures for the meatballs are given separately in case you want to serve them with other dishes.

In a large saucepan over medium heat, mix together onion, garlic, cumin, tomato sauce, and stock; bring to a boil. Reduce heat to low; add Mexican Meatballs and simmer, covered, until meatballs are thoroughly cooked (about 40 minutes).

Just before serving, add lemon juice; taste and adjust seasoning if necessary. For a spicier soup, add hot-pepper sauce.

Makes 8 cups, eight 1-cup servings

SAUCES, GRAVIES, AND CONDIMENTS

Sir Humphrey Davy
Detested gravy.
He lived in the odium
Of having discovered sodium.

Edmund Clerihew Bentley (1875–1956)

When I wrote The Calculating Cook, *I stated in the introduction to the chapter on sauces that I felt like a sorcerer trying to make sauces taste like something they really were not. Now I realize I was only a sorcerer's apprentice, because creating sauces without salt and other high-sodium ingredients has taken a great deal more imagination and infinitely more hours of testing than anything I have ever done. I am delighted with the results, however, and hope you will share my enthusiasm for the sauce recipes given here, which will help improve the overall flavor of a low-sodium diet.*

Defatted Drippings

If you don't eat gravy because it is greasy, simply defat the drippings. All drippings are defatted in the same way. After cooking roast beef, leg of lamb, chicken, turkey, or other meat or poultry, remove it from the roasting pan and pour the drippings into a bowl. Refrigerate the bowl until the drippings are cold and all the fat has solidified on the top. Remove and discard the fat and you have defatted drippings.

If you are in a hurry for the drippings because you want to serve them with your roast, place them in the freezer instead of the refrigerator and place the roast in a warm oven to keep it from cooling. After the fat solidifies (about 20 minutes), you can remove it, heat the drippings, and serve.

When I roast meat or poultry, I always defat the drippings and keep them in the freezer. Defatted drippings add extra flavor to stocks and are better than stocks for making calorie-reduced gravies.

Unsalted Chicken Gravy

Each serving contains 22 calories, no cholesterol, 1 g fat, and negligible sodium

1 tablespoon unsalted corn oil
  margarine
2 tablespoons minced onion
1 cup thinly sliced fresh
  mushrooms (¹/₄ lb)
2 cups defatted chicken
  drippings (page 29)
2 cups Unsalted Chicken Stock
  (see page 17)
3 tablespoons cornstarch or
  arrowroot
¹/₄ cup cold water
Freshly ground black pepper,
  to taste
Freshly squeezed lemon juice
  (optional)

You will be both amazed and delighted that a gravy this rich tasting is so low in fat, calories, and sodium. I often add cooked chicken or turkey (see variation) to it and serve it over rice or pasta as an entrée.

In a skillet over medium heat, melt margarine. Add onion and cook until onion is tender. Add mushrooms and continue cooking until mushrooms are tender.

In a medium saucepan over medium heat, warm drippings and stock. Dissolve cornstarch in the water and add to stock mixture. Cook slowly, stirring occasionally, until mixture thickens slightly (3 to 5 minutes).

Add onion mixture to gravy and season with pepper and a little lemon juice (if desired).

Makes 4 cups, sixteen ¹/₄-cup servings

Unsalted Turkey Gravy
Substitute turkey drippings for the chicken drippings, and Unsalted Turkey Stock (see page 17) for the chicken stock.

Unsalted Beef Gravy

Each serving contains 18 calories, no cholesterol, no fat, and negligible sodium

2 tablespoons cornstarch or
  arrowroot
1 cup Unsalted Beef Stock
  (see page 16), chilled
1 cup defatted beef drippings
  (see page 29)
1 tablespoon dried onion flakes
Freshly ground black pepper,
  to taste
Dash hot-pepper sauce (optional)

This flavorsome gravy is easy to make. If you want a little more taste and texture, add minced onion and thinly sliced mushrooms that have been sautéed in unsalted corn oil margarine.

In a small bowl, dissolve cornstarch in ¹/₄ cup of the stock. In a medium saucepan over medium heat, warm drippings and remaining stock. Add cornstarch mixture to stock mixture and cook, stirring occasionally, until mixture thickens.

Add onion flakes, pepper, and hot-pepper sauce (if desired).

Makes about 1¹/₂ cups, six ¹/₄-cup servings

Unsalted Cocktail Sauce

Each serving contains 14 calories, no cholesterol, no fat, and 8 mg sodium

1 can (8 oz) unsalted tomato sauce
2 tablespoons freshly squeezed lemon juice
1 teaspoon grated fresh or unsalted prepared horseradish
Dash hot-pepper sauce

Serve this cocktail sauce over cold cooked fish and seafood to jazz them up. It is also delicious as a low-calorie dip for raw vegetables or as a spread for fish sandwiches.

In a small bowl combine all ingredients and mix well. Store, tightly covered, in the refrigerator.

Makes 1 cup, eight 2-tablespoon servings

Mexican Cocktail Sauce

Each serving contains 11 calories, no cholesterol, no fat, and 5 mg sodium

1 can (8 oz) unsalted tomato sauce
2 tablespoons freshly squeezed lemon juice
1/4 cup minced onion
1/2 cup finely chopped cilantro
Dash hot-pepper sauce

To add zest to cold fish or seafood, eggs, tacos, and grilled foods of all types, serve them with this cilantro-flavored low-sodium cocktail sauce.

In a small bowl combine all ingredients and mix well. Store, tightly covered, in the refrigerator.

Makes about 1^1/$_2$ cups, twelve 2-tablespoon servings

Marinara Sauce

Each serving contains 66 calories, no cholesterol, 1 g fat, and 36 mg sodium

1 tablespoon extra virgin olive
    oil
1 medium onion, peeled and
    finely chopped (1½ cups)
1 clove garlic, minced
4 cans (8 oz each) unsalted
    tomato sauce
2 cans (6 oz each) unsalted
    tomato paste (1½ cups)
1 quart water
¼ teaspoon freshly ground
    black pepper
1 teaspoon each dried oregano
    and dried basil, crushed
1 bay leaf

I keep some of this sauce in the refrigerator or freezer for emergencies, such as unexpected dinner guests. I simply heat it, pour it over any kind of pasta I happen to have on hand, and toss a salad with a little Secret Basic Dressing (see page 45)—a gourmet meal in minutes.

In a heavy skillet over medium heat, warm oil. Add onion and garlic and sauté until they are soft and golden brown in color.

Add tomato sauce, tomato paste, water, pepper, oregano, basil, and bay leaf; mix thoroughly. Bring mixture to a boil, reduce heat, and simmer, uncovered, at least 2 hours. To store sauce, transfer to a nonmetallic container and refrigerate or freeze.

Makes 7 cups, fourteen ½-cup servings

Mustard Sauce

Each serving contains 49 calories, negligible cholesterol, 3 g fat, and 22 mg sodium

4 teaspoons ground mustard
¼ cup cider vinegar
3 egg whites, slightly beaten
½ cup nonfat milk
2 tablespoons unsalted corn oil
    margarine
3 tablespoons sugar

This sauce is equally good, either hot or cold, on fish, poultry, or meat. It makes a special dressing for potato salad and a savory topping for baked potatoes.

In a small saucepan combine mustard and vinegar; stir until mustard is completely dissolved. Add egg whites and milk and stir to blend. Place mixture over low heat and slowly bring to a boil, stirring constantly with a wire whisk. Continue cooking and stirring for 30 seconds after mixture begins to boil.

Remove pan from heat and place margarine on surface of mixture. Do not stir. Allow to cool to room temperature. Add sugar and mix thoroughly with a wire whisk. Store in the refrigerator.

Makes 1¼ cups, ten 2-tablespoon servings

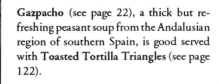

Gazpacho (see page 22), a thick but refreshing peasant soup from the Andalusian region of southern Spain, is good served with **Toasted Tortilla Triangles** (see page 122).

Major Jones Chutney (see page 40) is a perfect accompaniment to **Indian Lamb Curry** (see page 115), served over rice and garnished with peanuts, green onion, and lemon zest.

Timing is the most important element in preparing **Chinese Snow Pea and Shrimp Salad**, shown here sprinkled with sesame seeds (see page 53).

Pineapple Muffins (see page 128) make a hearty accompaniment to a luncheon soup or salad, a delicious after-school snack, or a quick breakfast on the run.

Unsalted White Sauce

Each serving contains 110 calories, 3 mg cholesterol, 3 g fat, and 96 mg sodium

3 cups nonfat milk
1 tablespoon unsalted corn oil
   margarine
3 tablespoons flour
¹/₈ teaspoon ground white
   pepper

This method of making white or béchamel sauce is easy and almost foolproof. The ratio of fat to flour is much lower in this recipe than in the classic version, so it takes a little longer to thicken, but the few extra minutes are well worth the effort. If lumps form in the sauce, simply pour it into a blender and blend until smooth.

In a medium saucepan over low heat, cook milk until it simmers.

In another saucepan over low heat, melt margarine; add flour, stirring constantly, and cook for 3 minutes. Do not allow mixture to brown.

Remove flour-margarine mixture from heat and add simmering milk all at once, stirring continuously with a wire whisk. Return sauce to low heat and cook slowly until thickened (about 30 minutes), stirring occasionally. (If you want a thicker sauce, cook it a little longer.) Add pepper and stir well.

Makes 1¹/₃ cups, four ¹/₃-cup servings

Unsalted Light Brown Sauce

Each serving contains 21 calories, no cholesterol, no fat, and 2 mg sodium

4 cups Unsalted Beef Stock
   (see page 16)
2 tablespoons finely chopped
   shallot
$1/2$ cup red table wine
$1/4$ cup dry sherry
$1/4$ cup dry white wine
   (I prefer Chablis)
4 tablespoons cornstarch
$1/4$ cup cold water
$1/2$ teaspoon freshly ground
   black pepper
Dash hot-pepper sauce

Because this low-sodium version of French brown sauce lacks the rich, dark brown color associated with the classic sauce, it is called light. *The distinctive darkness of the classic sauce is obtained either by adding caramel coloring, which is difficult to find though perfectly acceptable in a low-sodium diet, or Kitchen Bouquet flavoring, which is high in sodium.*

In a medium saucepan over medium heat, cook stock until warm.

In another medium saucepan over fairly high heat, combine shallot, red wine, sherry, and white wine; boil until mixture is reduced by one third. Add warm stock, reduce heat to medium, and cook mixture until it simmers.

Mix cornstarch with the water until cornstarch is completely dissolved. Add to the sauce, mixing thoroughly with a wire whisk. Add pepper and hot-pepper sauce. Stir until blended and thickened to desired consistency.

Makes $4^1/3$ cups, thirteen $1/3$-cup servings

Sauce Hollandaise Sans Sel

Each serving contains 133 calories, 71 mg cholesterol, 13 g fat, and 37 mg sodium

2 egg yolks (see page 164)
2 tablespoons freshly squeezed
   lemon juice
Pinch cayenne pepper
6 tablespoons unsalted corn oil
   margarine, melted
3 egg whites (see page 164)
$^1/_8$ teaspoon cream of tartar

Adding egg whites to hollandaise sauce lightens the texture and doubles the yield, so that each serving has fewer calories. This sauce is delicious on vegetables, poached fish, and poultry, and it is an essential ingredient for Eggs Benedict (see page 78).

In a blender combine egg yolks, lemon juice, and cayenne. Cover and blend at high speed for 2 to 3 seconds. Reduce speed to medium, remove lid but leave blender running, and slowly add melted margarine in a very thin stream. (If sauce will not be used immediately, set blender container in a pan of lukewarm water so that sauce will not separate.)

In a small mixing bowl, combine egg whites and cream of tartar and beat until stiff but not dry, then fold into sauce mixture until sauce is smooth but still very light textured. If desired, reheat in a double boiler over simmering water.

Makes 1$^1/_2$ cups, six $^1/_4$-cup servings

Sauce Béarnaise Sans Sel

Each serving contains 139 calories, 71 mg cholesterol, 14 g fat, and 38 mg sodium

1/4 cup red wine vinegar
1/4 cup dry white wine
1 tablespoon minced shallot or green onion top
2 teaspoons dried tarragon, crushed
1/8 teaspoon freshly ground black pepper
Pinch cayenne pepper
2 egg yolks (see page 164)
6 tablespoons unsalted corn oil margarine, melted
3 egg whites (see page 164)
1/8 teaspoon cream of tartar
2 tablespoons minced parsley

The egg whites do the same thing for béarnaise sauce that they do for hollandaise sauce—lighten the texture and double the yield, thereby reducing the number of calories per serving. The stronger flavor of béarnaise makes it a superb sauce for meat.

In a small saucepan combine vinegar, wine, shallot, tarragon, black pepper, and cayenne. Place over fairly high heat and boil until mixture is reduced to 2 tablespoons. Remove from heat and let cool to room temperature.

In a blender container combine egg yolks and cooled vinegar mixture. Cover and blend at high speed for 2 seconds. Reduce speed to medium, remove lid but leave blender running, and slowly add melted margarine in a very thin stream. (If sauce will not be used immediately, set blender container in a pan of lukewarm water so that sauce will not separate.)

In a small mixing bowl, combine egg whites and cream of tartar and beat until stiff but not dry. Fold egg whites and parsley into sauce mixture until sauce is smooth but still very light textured. If desired, reheat in a double boiler over simmering water.

Makes 1 1/2 cups, six 1/4-cup servings

Unsalted Mayonnaise

Each serving contains 128 calories, 14 mg cholesterol, 14 g fat, and 5 mg sodium

1 egg
1 teaspoon ground mustard
Pinch cayenne pepper
1 tablespoon freshly squeezed
    lemon juice
1¹/₂ teaspoons red wine vinegar
1 cup corn or extra virgin olive
    oil

You may never want to go back to using a commercial product after you taste this mayonnaise, which is better than any other mayonnaise I have ever tasted. I vary the oil, depending on what I am using the mayonnaise for. For a fruit salad I use corn oil, but for almost everything else I prefer the stronger flavor of an extra virgin olive oil.

Dip whole egg in the shell in boiling water for 30 seconds. Remove egg from the water and break into a blender container. Add mustard and cayenne, cover container, and blend at high speed until mixture is thick and foamy (about 30 seconds). Add lemon juice and vinegar and blend for a few more seconds to mix.

Reduce blender speed to medium, remove lid but leave blender running, and slowly add oil into exact center of container in a very thin stream (see Note). Blend only until thick and creamy (about 3 minutes). Store, tightly covered, in the refrigerator.

Makes 1 cup, sixteen 1-tablespoon servings

> *NOTE* It is extremely important to add oil very slowly so mayonnaise does not separate. If it does, place a very small amount of separated mayonnaise in a warmed mixing bowl and beat with a wire whisk until it starts to thicken. Add remaining separated mayonnaise, 1 teaspoon at a time, continuing to beat with whisk until mixture thickens.

Secret Tartar Sauce

Each serving contains 31 calories, 5 mg cholesterol, 3 g fat, and 5 mg sodium

⅓ cup light sour cream
2 tablespoons Unsalted
   Mayonnaise (see page 37)
1½ teaspoons freshly squeezed
   lemon juice
¼ teaspoon sugar
2 tablespoons Dilled Onion
   Relish (see page 40)

Not only is this tartar sauce lower in sodium than most other tartar sauces, it is also lower in calories. No one will guess those secrets, though: It is richer and more piquant than most salty, high-fat versions.

In a small mixing bowl, combine sour cream, mayonnaise, lemon juice, and sugar; mix well. Add relish and mix thoroughly. Store, tightly covered, in the refrigerator.

Makes 1 cup, sixteen 1-tablespoon servings

Low-Sodium Dill Sauce

Each serving contains 97 calories, 10 mg cholesterol, 10 g fat, and 18 mg sodium

½ cup Unsalted Mayonnaise
   (see page 37)
1 cup nonfat plain yogurt
1 teaspoon dried tarragon,
   crushed
1½ teaspoons dried dill weed,
   crushed
1 teaspoon freshly squeezed
   lemon juice

Always try to make this sauce the day before you plan to use it; the flavor is stronger when the sauce is allowed to stand for 24 hours. Dill sauce enhances vegetables and seafood. It is a special favorite on sliced cucumbers, and it is a key ingredient in my recipe for Salmon Quenelles (see page 92).

In a small mixing bowl, combine mayonnaise and yogurt and blend thoroughly with a wire whisk. Add tarragon, dill, and lemon juice; mix well. Pour sauce into a container with a tight-fitting lid and refrigerate.

Makes about 1½ cups, twelve 2-tablespoon servings

Asian Sesame Seed Sauce
Each serving contains 90 calories, no cholesterol, 9 g fat, and negligible sodium

1/3 cup corn oil
1/3 cup dark sesame oil
2 tablespoons freshly squeezed lemon juice
2 tablespoons dry sherry
2 tablespoons sugar
1 clove garlic, minced

Try this versatile sauce as a salad dressing, as a marinade for fish or chicken, or as a sauce for fruit, vegetables, fish, meat, or poultry. Thickened with a little pectin, it can be used as a dip for raw or cold cooked vegetables. Note that sauce must be chilled for 24 hours before using.

In a jar with a tight-fitting lid, combine all ingredients and mix well, shaking vigorously for 1 full minute. Place in the refrigerator for at least 24 hours before using. Before each use it is important to shake the sauce container vigorously to ensure that sauce is well blended.

Makes about 1 cup, sixteen 1-tablespoon servings

Lemon Barbecue Sauce
Each serving contains 68 calories, no cholesterol, 7 g fat, and negligible sodium

1/2 cup freshly squeezed lemon juice
1/2 teaspoon freshly ground black pepper
1 teaspoon smoke flavoring
1 teaspoon dried thyme, crushed
2 tablespoons grated onion
2 cloves garlic, minced
1/4 cup corn oil

This is an excellent barbecue sauce for fish and poultry. As a marinade for meat, it helps to tenderize the meat as well as season it delightfully. It is best prepared at least 24 hours before using.

In a small mixing bowl, combine lemon juice, pepper, smoke flavoring, and thyme; mix well. Add onion, garlic, and oil and mix thoroughly. Cover and refrigerate for at least 24 hours before using.

Makes about 1 cup, eight 2-tablespoon servings

Major Jones Chutney

Each serving contains 45 calories, no cholesterol, negligible fat, and 3 mg sodium

3/4 pound tart green apples, unpeeled, cored, and finely chopped (2 cups)
1 cup finely chopped raisins
1 teaspoon corn oil
1 teaspoon ground mustard or crushed whole mustard seed
1 teaspoon ground coriander
3/4 teaspoon each ground ginger and chili powder
1/4 teaspoon each ground turmeric, ground cumin, and garlic powder
1/8 teaspoon cayenne pepper
2 1/2 tablespoons red wine vinegar
1 1/2 cups water

Because commercial chutney is high in sodium, often containing almost 600 milligrams of sodium per two-tablespoon serving, this chutney is a welcomed accompaniment to any low-sodium meal.

In a large mixing bowl, combine apples and raisins; mix thoroughly and set aside.

In a heavy saucepan over low heat, heat the oil. Add mustard, coriander, ginger, chili powder, turmeric, cumin, garlic powder, and cayenne; mix well. Combine vinegar and the water and add to spice mixture; increase heat to medium and bring mixture to a boil. Add reserved apple-raisin mixture and cook, uncovered, over low heat until liquid is absorbed and apples are completely tender (about 1 1/4 hours), stirring occasionally.

Remove from heat and let cool to room temperature. Store in a covered container in the refrigerator.

Makes 2 cups, sixteen 2-tablespoon servings

Dilled Onion Relish

Each serving contains 84 calories, no cholesterol, negligible fat, and 5 mg sodium

1 cup distilled white vinegar
3/4 cup sugar
1 tablespoon dried dill weed, crushed
1/4 cup water
4 medium white onions, peeled and finely chopped (6 cups)
1 large green bell pepper, seeded and finely chopped (1 cup)
1 jar (4 oz) pimientos, drained and finely chopped

The uses for this relish are limited only by your imagination. It is good with cold meats, fish, and poultry, in salads, and on sandwiches. I use it instead of salad dressing in tuna salad, and it is fabulous. Note that relish must be chilled for two days before using.

In a small bowl combine vinegar and sugar; stir until sugar is completely dissolved. Add dill and the water and mix well; set aside.

In a large jar combine onions, bell pepper, and pimientos; add vinegar mixture, cover with a tight-fitting lid, and shake jar until ingredients are thoroughly mixed. Refrigerate for 2 days before serving.

Makes about 6 cups, twelve 1/2-cup servings

Honey "Butter"

Each serving contains 72 calories, no cholesterol, 2 g fat, and 2 mg sodium

¹/₄ cup unsalted corn oil margarine, at room temperature
1 cup spun honey, at room temperature

Try this ambrosial spread on toast, pancakes, waffles, and French toast, and drizzle it on fresh fruit or ice cream. It also turns popcorn into a marvelous dessert.

In a small bowl combine margarine and honey; mix thoroughly.

Makes 1¹/₄ cups, twenty 1-tablespoon servings

Low-Sodium Jelled Milk

Each serving contains 14 calories, negligible cholesterol, no fat, and 17 mg sodium

1 envelope (1 scant tablespoon) unflavored gelatin
2 tablespoons cold water
¹/₄ cup boiling water
1 cup nonfat milk

The thick, creamy consistency of jelled milk makes it a perfect topping for cereals and fruits. You can also use it instead of ice cream as a base for milk shakes to cut the calories without giving up the rich thickness.

In a small bowl soften gelatin in the cold water. Add the boiling water and stir until gelatin is completely dissolved. Add milk and mix well. Place in a covered container in the refrigerator; when mixture is jelled, it is ready to use.

Makes 1 cup, eight 2-tablespoon servings

Sherry-Ginger Sauce

1/4 cup dry sherry
1 tablespoon cornstarch
1 tablespoon cider vinegar
1 clove garlic, minced
1/8 teaspoon ground ginger
1 teaspoon sugar
1/2 cup Unsalted Beef Stock (see page 16)

In a small saucepan combine sherry, cornstarch, vinegar, garlic, ginger, and sugar; stir until cornstarch is completely dissolved. Add stock and cook over low heat until sauce is thickened, stirring constantly.

Makes about 2/3 cup

Brandy Sauce

1/2 cup firmly packed brown sugar
1 tablespoon unsalted corn oil margarine
1/2 cup canned evaporated skimmed milk
1 tablespoon brandy or 1 teaspoon brandy extract

In a 1-quart saucepan over medium heat, combine all ingredients. Cook, stirring often, until mixture comes to a full boil (3 to 4 minutes).

Makes about 1/2 cup

Vanilla Sauce

1/2 cup light sour cream
1 1/2 teaspoons sugar
1/2 teaspoon vanilla extract

In a small bowl combine all ingredients; mix with a wire whisk.

Makes 1/2 cup

SALAD DRESSINGS

A great salad requires a great salad dressing. A good-tasting, low-sodium salad dressing is as difficult to achieve as a flavorful low-sodium sauce. In the "secret" salad dressings in this chapter (see pages 44 to 48), I call for a wide variety of herbs and spices to appeal to a range of tastes. An important bonus of salt-free salad dressing is that you can dress salads hours before serving them without having the lettuce wilt and become soggy. Salt is what draws the moisture from the greens, causing them to lose their crispness.

Before you dress any salad with one of my dressings, be sure to wash and dry the salad greens thoroughly. This is important for two reasons: First, no one likes a gritty salad; and second, wet greens dilute the dressing, making it seem less flavorful.

You will find that most of the salad dressings in this section actually improve with age: The ingredients blend together for a smoother flavor. If allowed to stand undisturbed for very long, however, any dressing tends to separate; therefore, be sure to shake or stir vigorously before each use.

Many of these salad dressings also make excellent marinades for cold cooked vegetables, fish, meat, and poultry. For maximum flavor, poultry and red meats are best marinated in the refrigerator for at least 24 hours before cooking.

Secret Caesar Dressing

Each serving contains 50 calories, 3 mg cholesterol, 4 g fat, and 73 mg sodium

2 tablespoons extra virgin
　　olive oil
1 clove garlic
1/2 ounce anchovy fillets
　　(3 fillets), very well rinsed
　　and finely chopped
1 egg
1/4 teaspoon freshly ground
　　black pepper
2 tablespoons freshly squeezed
　　lemon juice
1 tablespoon low-sodium
　　Worcestershire sauce
2 teaspoons red wine vinegar
1/4 cup freshly grated Parmesan
　　cheese

This dressing is so good that many Caesar salad buffs have no idea they are eating a low-sodium preparation. You may want to keep the ingredients your secret.

In a skillet over low heat, warm oil. With a garlic press, squeeze garlic into oil and cook until garlic just sizzles; do not brown. Remove from heat and allow to cool.

Add anchovy to oil mixture and mix well; set aside.

Dip whole egg in shell into boiling water for 30 seconds. Separate egg; discard yolk and add egg white to oil mixture. Blend well.

Add remaining ingredients; mix well. Store, tightly covered, in the refrigerator.

Makes 1/2 cup, eight 1-tablespoon servings

Fiesta Dressing

Each serving contains 12 calories, no cholesterol, no fat, and 6 mg sodium

1 can (16 oz) unsalted stewed
　　tomatoes
1/4 cup freshly squeezed lemon
　　juice
2 tablespoons red wine vinegar
3 tablespoons finely chopped
　　onion
2 cloves garlic, chopped
1/4 teaspoon each chili powder
　　and ground cumin
1/4 teaspoon dried oregano,
　　crushed
1/4 teaspoon freshly ground
　　black pepper
1/8 teaspoon hot-pepper sauce

For anyone watching calories as well as sodium, this oil-free dressing is perfect. If you chop the ingredients coarsely instead of blending them, you can serve the dressing as a sauce with fish, poultry, or meat.

In a blender container combine all ingredients and blend until smooth. Store, covered, in the refrigerator.

Makes 2 cups, sixteen 2-tablespoon servings

Secret Basic Dressing

Each serving contains 14 calories, no cholesterol, 1 g fat, and negligible sodium

¹/₄ cup red wine vinegar
1 clove garlic, minced
¹/₄ teaspoon ground mustard
¹/₂ teaspoon sugar
³/₄ cup water
¹/₄ teaspoon freshly ground
    black pepper
2 tablespoons freshly squeezed
    lemon juice
2 tablespoons corn oil

This will be the most important salad dressing in the refrigerator. After experimenting with the variations suggested here, you can create others and develop your own "house" dressing. I always pass a large pepper mill around the table, suggesting to my guests that freshly ground black pepper rather than salt can be used when a salad seems to be missing something.

In a small bowl combine vinegar, garlic, mustard, and sugar; stir until dry ingredients are thoroughly dissolved. Add the water, black pepper, and lemon juice; mix well. Slowly stir in oil.

Pour mixture into a jar with a tight-fitting lid and shake vigorously for 2 full minutes. Store, covered, in the refrigerator.

Makes 1 ¹/₄ cups, twenty 1-tablespoon servings

Secret Curry Dressing
To Secret Basic Dressing add ¹/₂ teaspoon curry powder and ¹/₈ teaspoon ground ginger.

Secret Tarragon Dressing
To Secret Basic Dressing add 1 tablespoon crushed dried tarragon.

Secret Cumin Dressing
To Secret Basic Dressing add ¹/₂ teaspoon ground cumin and ¹/₈ teaspoon chili powder.

Secret Fennel Dressing
To Secret Basic Dressing add 1 teaspoon crushed fennel seed.

Continued on page 46—

Secret Italian Dressing

To Secret Basic Dressing add $1/2$ teaspoon sugar, 2 teaspoons crushed dried oregano, and 1 teaspoon each crushed dried basil and dried tarragon. This adds 1 calorie to Secret Basic Dressing.

Secret Vinaigrette Dressing

To Secret Basic Dressing add 2 tablespoons each chopped pimiento, finely chopped chives, and finely chopped parsley; 2 finely chopped hard-cooked egg whites; $1/8$ teaspoon paprika; and dash hot-pepper sauce. This adds 2 calories and 5 mg sodium to Secret Basic Dressing, and increases the yield to $1^1/2$ cups, twenty-four 1-tablespoon servings.

Celery Seed Dressing

Each serving contains 19 calories, no cholesterol, 1 g fat, and negligible sodium

2 tablespoons sugar
$1/4$ cup tarragon white-wine vinegar
2 tablespoons freshly squeezed lemon juice
$1/4$ teaspoon freshly ground black pepper
$1/2$ teaspoon onion powder
$3/4$ cup water
$1^1/2$ teaspoons celery seed, crushed
2 tablespoons corn oil

This dressing is good on fruits as well as vegetables. I particularly like it on tuna salad to which apples and raisins have been added. Be sure to shake the dressing container vigorously before each use.

In a small bowl dissolve sugar in vinegar. Add lemon juice, pepper, onion powder, the water, and celery seed; mix thoroughly. Slowly stir in oil.

Pour mixture into a jar with a tight-fitting lid and shake vigorously for a full minute. Store, covered, in the refrigerator.

Makes $1^1/4$ cups, twenty 1-tablespoon servings

Orange-Onion Dressing

Each serving contains 16 calories, no cholesterol, 1 g fat, and negligible sodium

$1/4$ cup rice vinegar
$1/2$ teaspoon sugar
$1/4$ teaspoon ground mustard
$1/4$ cup freshly squeezed orange
  juice
$1/4$ teaspoon freshly ground
  black pepper
$1/2$ medium onion, peeled and
  chopped ($3/4$ cup)
1 tablespoon corn oil
1 tablespoon dark sesame oil

Try marinating chicken breasts in this dressing for about 3 hours, broiling them, and then serving the warm chicken over a salad tossed with this same dressing and garnished with toasted sesame seed.

In a blender container place vinegar, sugar, mustard, orange juice, pepper, and onion; blend until onion is liquefied.
    Pour mixture into a jar with a tight-fitting lid and add oils. Cover jar and shake vigorously for 30 seconds. Store, covered, in the refrigerator.

Makes 1¼ cups, twenty 1-tablespoon servings

Banana Cream Dressing

Each serving contains 36 calories, 1 mg cholesterol, negligible fat, and 30 mg sodium

2 small ripe bananas ($1/2$ lb),
  sliced (about $1^1/2$ cups)
1 teaspoon freshly squeezed
  lemon juice
2 cups nonfat plain yogurt
1 teaspoon coconut extract
$1/2$ teaspoon vanilla extract

This is a fabulous fat-free dressing for fruit salad. I like it best over a salad containing fresh pineapple or pineapple canned only in its natural juices.

In a blender container place bananas and lemon juice and blend until smooth. Add yogurt and coconut and vanilla and blend again until smooth. Store, covered, in the refrigerator.

Makes 3 cups, twelve ¼-cup servings

Curried Ginger Dressing

Each serving contains 35 calories, 7 mg cholesterol, 4 g fat, and 5 mg sodium

1 cup light sour cream
$^1/_4$ cup Unsalted Mayonnaise
   (see page 37)
$^3/_4$ teaspoon curry powder
$^1/_4$ teaspoon ground ginger
2 teaspoons freshly squeezed
   lemon juice

Besides enhancing a green salad, this dressing makes an excellent sauce for fish or poultry and a delicious spread for meat sandwiches.

In a blender container combine all ingredients and blend until smooth. Store, covered, in the refrigerator.

Makes 1$^1/_4$ cups, twenty 1-tablespoon servings

Curried Coconut Dressing
To Curried Ginger Dressing add $^1/_2$ teaspoon coconut extract.

Curried Applesauce Dressing

Each serving contains 47 calories, no cholesterol, 5 g fat, and negligible sodium

$^3/_4$ cup unsweetened applesauce
2 tablespoons freshly squeezed
   lemon juice
1 tablespoon rice vinegar
$^1/_2$ teaspoon each vanilla extract
   and ground cinnamon
$^1/_4$ teaspoon curry powder
$^1/_8$ teaspoon ground ginger
$^1/_2$ cup corn oil

Like the Curried Ginger Dressing above, this dressing makes an unusual sauce. I omitted the oil and served it instead of cranberry sauce for Thanksgiving, and everyone loved it.

In a small bowl combine applesauce, lemon juice, vinegar, vanilla, cinnamon, curry powder, and ginger; mix thoroughly. Add oil and mix well. Store, covered, in the refrigerator.

Makes about 1$^1/_2$ cups, twenty-four 1-tablespoon servings

SALADS

When planning a menu, take advantage of the great versatility of salads. Light, low-calorie salads can be served before, with, or after an entrée; hearty salads, which can include all the nutrition necessary for a balanced meal, can be served as the main course. With the variety of flavors and textures that salads provide, you will find that they give more satisfaction for fewer calories than any other item on your menu.

Make it a habit to save a few extra minutes for decorating your salads, and always serve them on chilled plates. When using lettuce or other greens, wash them thoroughly a couple of hours before you plan to serve the salad. Pat the greens dry with paper towels, tear them into bite-sized pieces, and place them in a colander. Place the colander on top of a plate to drain, and store in the refrigerator until serving time. Your salads will be crisper and require less salad dressing, because the dressing will not be diluted by unwanted water. And remember the big advantage of using salt-free salad dressing: You can dress the salad hours before serving time and it won't wilt. You can also store leftover salad, and prepare make-ahead lunches, without worrying about soggy greens!

Curried Orange Appetizer

Each serving contains 109 calories, no cholesterol, 3 g fat, and 2 mg sodium

6 large oranges (3 lb), peeled
    and thinly sliced (7 cups)
1 cup Secret Curry Dressing
    (see page 45)
1 large onion, peeled and diced
    (2 cups)
Parsley sprigs, for garnish

Attractive and easy to serve, this is an ideal appetizer, salad, or cold course for a buffet. Red onion makes the presentation even more colorful.

In a glass baking dish spread orange slices and pour dressing over them. Sprinkle onion evenly over orange slices, cover dish, and refrigerate for at least 3 hours before serving. Serve on chilled plates and garnish with parsley sprigs.

Makes 8 cups, eight 1-cup servings

Mystery Slaw

Each serving contains 77 calories, no cholesterol, negligible fat, and 11 mg sodium

1 can (20 oz) unsweetened
    crushed pineapple,
    undrained
1 teaspoon sugar
1¹/₂ teaspoons coconut extract
1 head cauliflower, finely
    grated (about 4 cups)
Ground cinnamon, for
    sprinkling
Mint sprigs, for garnish
    (optional)

Many of your guests will think that they are eating shredded fresh coconut and pineapple, hence the "mystery" in the name of this salad.

Into a large bowl pour juice from canned pineapple; reserve crushed pineapple. Add sugar and coconut extract to juice and mix until sugar is thoroughly dissolved. Add cauliflower and mix well; add pineapple and mix well again. Cover and refrigerate for at least 2 hours before serving.

Divide salad evenly among 4 chilled plates. Sprinkle each serving lightly with cinnamon. Garnish each with mint (if desired).

Makes 4 cups, six ²/₃-cup servings

Wilted Spanish Salad

Each serving contains 108 calories, no cholesterol, 11 g fat, and 11 mg sodium

3 tablespoons extra virgin olive
  oil
1/2 teaspoon ground cumin
1 clove garlic, minced
  (1 teaspoon)
1 tablespoon freshly squeezed
  lemon juice
Dash hot-pepper sauce
1 large head iceberg lettuce,
  finely shredded (about 8
  cups)

For variety use shredded spinach instead of lettuce, but be sure to remove the veins from each leaf to keep the salad from tasting bitter.

In a small saucepan over low heat, combine oil, cumin, and garlic; heat until oil mixture is hot enough to wilt lettuce. Add lemon juice and hot-pepper sauce to oil mixture; stir to blend. Pour over lettuce, toss thoroughly, and serve immediately.

Makes 6 cups, four 1 1/2-cup servings

Curry Condiment Salad

Each serving contains 170 calories, 9 mg cholesterol, 8 g fat, and 49 mg sodium

1 large head iceberg lettuce,
  torn into bite-sized pieces
  (about 8 cups)
1/4 cup raisins
4 hard-cooked egg whites,
  chopped
1 medium red apple unpeeled,
  cored, and diced (1 1/3 cups)
1 can (8 oz) unsweetened
  pineapple chunks, drained
1/2 cup Curried Coconut
  Dressing (see page 48)
1/4 cup finely chopped unsalted
  dry-roasted peanuts
Mint or parsley sprigs, for
  garnish

This salad contains many of the ingredients frequently served as condiments with curry dishes. I often add cooked fish or poultry to this salad and serve it as an entrée. It is also tasty with low-sodium water-packed canned tuna.

In a large bowl combine lettuce, raisins, egg whites, apple, pineapple, and dressing; toss thoroughly.

Divide salad evenly among 6 chilled plates. Sprinkle each serving with 2 teaspoons peanuts and garnish with mint.

Makes 10 cups, six 1 2/3-cup servings

Apple and Cheese Salad

Each serving contains 290 calories, 40 mg cholesterol, 21 g fat, and 14 mg sodium

1/2 cup chopped walnuts
1 large head iceberg lettuce, chopped (about 8 cups)
3 medium Delicious apples, unpeeled, cored and diced (about 4 cups)
1/2 pound low-sodium Monterey jack cheese, diced (2 cups)
3/4 cup Secret Italian Dressing (see page 46)

Of all the salads in the book, this is my favorite. It is similar to Jeanne's Appleseed Salad in my Fabulous Fiber Cookbook, *except here I use walnuts instead of sunflower seeds. The walnuts add more flavor, compensating for the greatly reduced sodium content of the salad.*

Preheat oven to 350° F. Toast walnuts on a baking sheet until they are golden brown (about 10 minutes). Watch carefully; they burn easily. Set aside.

In a large bowl combine lettuce, apples, cheese, and dressing; toss thoroughly. Divide evenly among 6 chilled plates. Sprinkle a rounded tablespoon of the toasted walnuts over each serving.

Makes 10 cups, six 1²/₃-cup servings

Pineapple and Cheese Salad

Each serving contains 372 calories, 60 mg cholesterol, 25 g fat, and 18 mg sodium

1/2 cup chopped walnuts
1 large head iceberg lettuce, finely chopped (about 8 cups)
1 can (20 oz) unsweetened crushed pineapple, drained
3/4 pound low-sodium Monterey jack cheese, diced (3 cups)
3/4 cup Orange-Onion Dressing (see page 47)

Serve this salad with Lettuce Bread (see page 125) for a light luncheon. It is also an appetizing accompaniment to roasted poultry or pork. For a variation try substituting toasted almonds for the walnuts.

Preheat oven to 350° F. Toast walnuts on a baking sheet until they are golden brown (about 10 minutes). Watch carefully; they burn easily. Set aside.

In a large bowl combine lettuce, pineapple, cheese, and dressing; toss thoroughly. Divide evenly among 6 chilled plates. Sprinkle a rounded tablespoon of the toasted walnuts over each serving.

Makes 10 cups, six 1²/₃-cup servings

East Indian Tuna Salad

Each serving contains 313 calories, 61 mg cholesterol, 16 g fat, and 61 mg sodium

6 small heads Boston lettuce
1 can (20 oz) unsweetened crushed pineapple, undrained
2 cans (6 ½ oz each) low-sodium, water-packed tuna, drained
½ cup raisins, finely chopped
¾ cup Curried Coconut Dressing (see page 48)

I like to serve this salad for a luncheon with Giant Cinnamon Popovers (see page 131) followed by Cold Orange Soufflé (see page 146) for dessert. After the holidays I make this salad with leftover cooked turkey instead of tuna.

Remove hearts from heads of lettuce, being careful not to separate or tear outer leaves. Wash hearts and tear into bite-sized pieces (about 8 cups). Place in a large bowl. Retain outer leaves for lettuce "bowls" in which to serve the salad. Wash leaves carefully and place on paper towels in the refrigerator until needed.

Add pineapple and its juice to torn lettuce. Separate tuna into bite-sized pieces and add to lettuce and pineapple. Add raisins and dressing; toss thoroughly.

Place each prepared lettuce bowl on a large chilled plate. Divide salad evenly among 6 bowls.

Makes 8 cups, six 1⅓-cup servings

Chinese Snow Pea and Shrimp Salad

Each serving contains 325 calories, 170 mg cholesterol, 20 g fat, and 173 mg sodium

1 small head cauliflower, separated into bite-sized florets (about 3 cups)
½ pound snow peas (3 cups)
1 pound peeled, deveined, cooked shrimp (about 3 cups), chilled
½ cup Asian Sesame Seed Sauce (see page 39)
sesame seeds, toasted, for garnish (optional)

Serve this salad for lunch with chopsticks. For a dish that is 61 milligrams lower in sodium than this shrimp version, substitute an equal amount of cooked chicken breast meat cut into julienne strips ¼ inch wide by 2 inches long.

In a large saucepan steam cauliflower over rapidly boiling water for 3 minutes. Add snow peas and cook until peas are just crisp-tender (2 minutes more). Remove from heat and immediately place vegetables under cold running water. Drain thoroughly and place in a large bowl. Cover and refrigerate until thoroughly chilled.

Add shrimp and sauce to vegetables and toss thoroughly. Sprinkle with toasted sesame seeds (if desired).

Makes 6 cups, four 1½-cup servings

Peanut-Mushroom Salad

Each serving contains 84 calories, 1 mg cholesterol, 6 g fat, and 21 mg sodium

$^1/_2$ pound fresh mushrooms, thinly sliced (2 cups)
2 tablespoons freshly squeezed lemon juice
$^3/_4$ cup nonfat milk
$^1/_2$ teaspoon sugar
$^3/_4$ teaspoon curry powder
$^1/_4$ teaspoon onion powder
Dash ground white pepper
1 tablespoon corn oil
1 large head Boston lettuce, torn into bite-sized pieces (4 to 5 cups)
$^1/_4$ cup chopped unsalted dry-roasted peanuts

This unlikely combination of ingredients is incredibly delicious. The salad is also good made with toasted pine nuts.

In a small nonmetallic bowl, combine mushrooms and lemon juice. Cover and refrigerate until ready to use.

In a small bowl combine milk, sugar, curry powder, onion powder, and pepper; mix thoroughly with a wire whisk to a creamy consistency. Beat in oil. Cover and refrigerate until ready to use.

Just before serving, toss together lettuce, marinated mushrooms, and dressing. Divide salad evenly among 6 chilled plates. Sprinkle 2 teaspoons chopped peanuts over each serving.

Makes 8 cups, six 1$^1/_3$-cup servings

Rainbow Chicken Salad

Each serving contains 267 calories, 73 mg cholesterol, 5 g fat, and 105 mg sodium

4 small heads Boston lettuce
3 boned, skinned chicken breasts (4 oz each), cooked and diced (2 cups)
1 cup chopped fresh pineapple or canned unsweetened pineapple chunks, drained
2 medium oranges, peeled and chopped (1 cup)
1 cup Banana Cream Dressing (see page 47)
1 cup fresh or unsweetened frozen blueberries, thawed
Ground cinnamon, for sprinkling

Lovely and delicious, this salad is a wonderful entrée for a light lunch or supper. Serve it with Gingerbread Muffins (see page 127) followed by Fast "Frozen" Yogurt (see page 141) for dessert.

Remove hearts from heads of lettuce, being careful not to separate or tear outer leaves. Wash hearts and tear into bite-sized pieces (about 5 cups). Place in a large bowl. Retain outer leaves for lettuce "bowls" in which to serve the salad. Wash leaves carefully and place on paper towels in the refrigerator until needed.

Add chicken, pineapple, oranges, and dressing to torn lettuce and toss thoroughly. Place each prepared lettuce bowl on a chilled salad plate and divide salad evenly among the bowls. Spoon $^1/_4$ cup blueberries on top of each serving, then sprinkle each salad lightly with cinnamon.

Makes 7 cups, four 1$^3/_4$-cup servings

St. Patrick's Day Potato Salad

Each serving contains 182 calories, no cholesterol, 7 g fat, and 9 mg sodium

2 pounds white potatoes (8 to
   10 small potatoes)
1 pound young green beans
$1/4$ cup dry vermouth
1 teaspoon freshly squeezed
   lemon juice
$1/4$ teaspoon freshly ground
   black pepper
$1/4$ cup extra virgin olive oil
$1/4$ cup finely sliced green onion,
   including tops
2 tablespoons minced fresh dill
   or 1 tablespoon dried dill
   weed, crushed
2 tablespoons finely chopped
   parsley
Parsley sprigs, for garnish

One of the few salads I prefer at room temperature rather than chilled, this is an inviting first course when served on lettuce leaves. With its touch of green, it is also a good vegetable side dish served with boiled beef for a St. Patrick's Day party.

In a large pot over medium heat, place potatoes and water to cover. Boil until just tender (20 to 25 minutes); do not overcook. Drain potatoes and allow them to cool until they can be handled easily.

Remove ends and strings from beans and cut each bean on the diagonal into 3 or 4 pieces. In a large saucepan steam beans over rapidly boiling water until they are crisp-tender (about 5 minutes). Remove beans from heat and immediately place under cold running water until thoroughly cool. Drain on a towel and set aside.

Peel cooled potatoes and cut lengthwise into $1/4$-inch-thick strips. Place strips in a large mixing bowl and set aside.

In a jar with a tight-fitting lid, shake vermouth, lemon juice, and pepper until well mixed. Add oil and shake vigorously for a full minute. Add green onion, dill, and chopped parsley and shake well again. Pour dressing over cooled potatoes and mix well; cover bowl and allow to stand for 1 hour at room temperature. Then add cooled green beans and toss thoroughly. Garnish with parsley sprigs. Serve at room temperature.

Makes 8 cups, eight 1-cup servings

Vegetarian Chef's Salad
Each serving contains 214 calories, 30 mg cholesterol, 15 g fat, and 21 mg sodium

¹/₄ cup raw sunflower seeds
¹/₂ large head iceberg lettuce, shredded (about 4 cups)
2 medium tomatoes, diced (1¹/₂ cups)
1 small stalk broccoli, florets only, chopped (1 cup)
¹/₂ cup each alfalfa sprouts and bean sprouts
¹/₄ pound low-sodium Cheddar cheese, diced (1 cup)
¹/₂ cup Secret Tarragon Dressing (see page 45)
Sprouts, for garnish (optional)

When sunflower sprouts are available, I use them to garnish this salad. When they're not in the market, I use any kind of sprout I can find.

Preheat oven to 350° F. Toast sunflower seeds on a baking sheet until they are golden brown (about 10 minutes). Watch carefully; they burn easily. Set aside.

In a large bowl combine lettuce, tomatoes, broccoli, sprouts, cheese, and dressing; toss thoroughly. Divide among 4 chilled plates. Sprinkle 1 tablespoon toasted sunflower seeds on each serving. Garnish with sprouts (if desired).

Makes 7 cups, four 1³/₄-cup servings

Pink Party Salad
Each serving contains 273 calories, 30 mg cholesterol, 20 g fat, and 36 mg sodium

2 tablespoons sliced almonds
1 medium red apple, unpeeled, diced (1 cup)
1 medium raw beet, peeled and shredded (1 cup)
¹/₄ pound low-sodium Monterey jack cheese, diced (1 cup)
¹/₂ large head iceberg lettuce, finely chopped (4 cups)
¹/₂ cup Curried Applesauce Dressing (see page 48)
4 leaves red cabbage

The ingredients in this salad are extremely complementary to each other. Unusual and interesting in combination, they tint the dressing pink. Whether or not you like pink, you'll love this salad

Preheat oven to 350° F. Toast almonds on a baking sheet until they are golden brown (8 to 10 minutes). Watch carefully; they burn easily. Set aside.

In a large bowl combine apple, beet, cheese, lettuce, and dressing; toss thoroughly. Place each cabbage leaf on a chilled plate and divide salad evenly among the leaves. Sprinkle each serving with 1¹/₂ teaspoons toasted almonds.

Makes 7 cups, four 1³/₄-cup servings

VEGETABLES

Vegetables play an important role in any modified diet program because they are low in calories and high in vitamins and minerals. However, there is an unusual paradox: Many of the vegetables that are lowest in calories and that are allowed in unlimited quantities in other diet programs are extremely high in sodium and must be restricted in the low-sodium diet. Two examples are celery and spinach. Although I have highlighted low-sodium vegetables in this chapter, I have included a few recipes using favorite high-sodium vegetables to show you how they can be incorporated in limited amounts—in keeping with my "never say 'never'" philosophy.

Many people claim that they are not particularly fond of vegetables in general, or of one vegetable in particular. Chances are that they have always been served vegetables that are either not fresh or are overcooked. Fresh vegetables that have been cooked properly are a treat for every sense. They are colorful and they provide an endless variety of textures and a wide range of flavors. That they are also very good for you makes them nature's most perfect food group.

Directions for Steaming Vegetables

When steaming vegetables, make certain that the level of the water is below the bottom of the steamer basket and that the water is boiling rapidly before the pot is covered and the timing is begun. Once the vegetables have steamed for the correct length of time, immediately place them under cold running water. This quickly stops the cooking and preserves both color and texture.

Whether vegetables are served hot or cold, they can be prepared ahead and stored, covered, in the refrigerator.

When reheating steamed vegetables, avoid overcooking them in the reheating process or they will lose both crispness and color.

Steaming Times for Fresh Vegetables

The time given for steaming each vegetable produces a crisp-tender result. Mushy, colorless vegetables not only are tasteless but also have been robbed of much of their nutritional value by overcooking.

Vegetable	Minutes
Artichokes	30
Asparagus	5
Beans	
Green	5
Lima	5
Snap	5
Bean sprouts	1 to 2
Beet greens	3 to 5
Beets, quartered	15
Breadfruit	10
Broccoli	5
Brussels sprouts	5
Cabbage, quartered	5
Carrots, 1/2-inch slices	5
Cauliflower	
Florets	3
Whole	5
Celery root	3 to 4
Celery stalks	10
Chard	1 to 2
Chayote	3
Chicory	1 to 2
Chives	2 to 3
Collard Greens	1 to 2
Corn	
Kernels	3
On the cob	3
Cucumbers	2 to 3
Dandelion greens	1 to 2
Eggplant, cut up	5
Green onions	3
Jerusalem artichokes	8
Jicama	10
Kale	1 to 2
Kohlrabi, quartered	8 to 10

Vegetable	Minutes
Leeks	5
Lettuce	1 to 2
Lotus root, 1/4-inch slices	25
Mushrooms	2
Mustard greens	1 to 2
Okra	5
Onions,	
Tops	3
Whole	5
Palm hearts	5
Peas	3 to 5
Peppers	
Chile	2 to 3
Green and red bell	2
Pimientos	2
Potatoes	
Sweet, 1/2-inch slices	15
White, 1/2-inch slices	10
Pumpkin, cut up	5
Radishes	
Black, 1/2-inch slices	5
Red, whole	5
Rhubarb	5
Rutabagas	8
Shallots	2
Snow peas	3
Spinach	1 to 2
Squash	
Acorn, cut up	5
Hubbard, cut up	5
Summer	3
Tomatoes	3
Turnips, quartered	8
Water chestnuts	8
Watercress	1 to 2

Broccoli Florets
Each serving contains 46 calories, no cholesterol, negligible fat, and 17 mg sodium

2 pounds broccoli (4 stalks)

Keep these florets in the refrigerator for a variety of uses. They make wonderful spur-of-the-moment hors d'oeuvres served with Low-Sodium Dill Sauce (see page 38) or Mustard Sauce (see page 32) for a dip.

Carefully remove broccoli florets from stalks, reserving stalks for Broccoli Stars (see page 60). In a large saucepan steam florets over rapidly boiling water until they are crisp-tender (5 minutes).

Remove from heat and place under cold running water. Drain thoroughly and chill if using for hors d'oeuvres or in a salad.

Makes 4 cups, four 1-cup servings

Green Bean Hors d'Oeuvre
Substitute 1 pound green beans for broccoli, remove and discard strings and ends from beans, and steam until beans are crisp-tender (5 minutes).

Makes 5 cups, ten ½-cup servings

Brussels Sprouts al Dente
Substitute 1 pound brussels sprouts (about 28 sprouts) for broccoli. Cut off and discard rough ends and any discolored leaves, and steam until sprouts are crisp-tender (10 minutes). Remove from heat and continue as directed.

Makes 4 cups, four 1-cup servings

Fresh Asparagus Tips
Substitute 1 pound asparagus (18 spears) for broccoli. Break off and discard tough end of each asparagus stalk by holding stalk in both hands and gently bending stem end until it breaks. Each stalk will break at a slightly different place depending on its toughness. In a large saucepan steam asparagus tips until crisp-tender (5 minutes). Remove from heat and continue as directed.

Makes 2 cups, four ½-cup servings

Broccoli Stars

Each serving contains 23 calories, no cholesterol, no fat, and 9 mg sodium

6 to 8 broccoli stalks (1 lb)

When you slice across a stalk of broccoli, you will see that each slice has a star pattern, which gives this dish its name. Just as the florets can be used in a variety of ways, so can the stars. They are great fun to serve because few people will know what they are, and they are economical because most people discard the stalks rather than create a "new" vegetable.

Slice broccoli stalks crosswise into 1/4-inch-thick stars. (You will have about 4 cups.) If you have a food processor, use it, because it is difficult to slice broccoli both thinly and evenly with a knife.

In a large saucepan steam stars over rapidly boiling water until they are crisp-tender (3 or 4 minutes). Remove from heat and rinse under cold running water. Drain thoroughly. Serve hot or chilled.

Makes 4 cups, eight 1/2-cup servings

Curried Broccoli Stars

Each serving contains 49 calories, no cholesterol, 3 g fat, and 10 mg sodium

2 tablespoons unsalted corn oil margarine
1/4 teaspoon curry powder
Dash ground white pepper
4 cups Broccoli Stars (see preceding recipe)

These curried stars are a wonderful taste accompaniment to grilled fish, poultry, or meat. A beautiful bright green color, they are also a decorative accent on the plate.

In a large saucepan over medium heat, melt margarine. Add curry powder and pepper and mix thoroughly. Add stars and heat thoroughly, stirring occasionally, but do not overcook or stars will lose their crispness and bright color.

Makes 4 cups, eight 1/2-cup servings

Tarragon-Cream Lettuce

Each serving contains 71 calories, 1 mg cholesterol, 2 g fat, and 52 mg sodium

1½ large heads iceberg lettuce, shredded (about 10 cups)
2 cups nonfat milk
1 tablespoon unsalted corn oil margarine
2½ tablespoons flour
⅛ teaspoon ground white pepper
2 teaspoons dried tarragon, crushed
2 teaspoons freshly squeezed lemon juice

If you have never had steamed lettuce, you're in for an unusual treat. It can be served warm as a side dish or chilled and served as a salad or condiment (see Note).

In a large saucepan over rapidly boiling water steam lettuce until just crisp-tender (about 1 minute). Immediately place under cold running water. Drain thoroughly and set aside.

In a small saucepan over low heat, heat milk until hot. In another small saucepan over low heat, melt margarine. Add flour to margarine and cook for 3 minutes, stirring constantly. Do not brown. Remove flour mixture from heat and add hot milk all at once, stirring constantly with a wire whisk. Return pan to low heat and cook mixture slowly for 20 to 30 minutes, stirring occasionally. Add pepper and tarragon; mix well. If sauce has any lumps, whirl in a blender until it is smooth. Add lemon juice and stir to blend well.

Transfer steamed lettuce to a large bowl and pour sauce over top. Toss thoroughly.

Makes 6 cups, six 1-cup servings

Note To serve chilled, refrigerate lettuce after draining it, and chill sauce before tossing it with lettuce.

Versatile Artichoke Bowls

Each serving contains 99 calories, no cholesterol, negligible fat, and 154 mg sodium

12 tiny artichokes (or 6 large
    artichokes)
1 tablespoon freshly squeezed
    lemon juice or vinegar

Artichokes are a versatile food that can be served hot or cold, by themselves or filled with other foods. For an appetizer serve tiny artichokes with a little Unsalted Mayonnaise (see page 37) spooned into the center of each. Or you can serve large artichokes on individual artichoke plates or dinner plates with Unsalted Mayonnaise on the side to use as a dip for the leaves. One of my favorite first courses is a large artichoke bowl filled with cold, jelled soup; I literally serve the soup in a salad. Filled with chicken or seafood salad, artichoke bowls are also beautiful cold luncheon entrées. For an unusual hot vegetable side dish, you can serve the artichoke bowls hot, filled with rice or an other-than-green, low-sodium vegetable. Hot artichoke bowls filled with warm fish, chicken, or meat also make a delicious entrée.

Wash artichokes well and pull off and discard tough outer leaves. Place artichokes in a nonaluminum container and cover with cold water to which lemon juice has been added. Let stand for 30 minutes or more (to force out any bugs that may be trapped in the leaves). Remove artichokes and discard water.

Holding each artichoke by the stem, cut tips off leaves with a pair of scissors, starting at bottom of artichoke and working to top in a spiral pattern. Trim stem even with bottom, turn artichoke upside down, and press firmly to open as much as possible.

Into a saucepan pour water to a depth of 2 inches and bring to a boil. Place trimmed artichokes in boiling water, cover tightly, and cook over medium heat until stems can be easily pierced with a fork (about 25 minutes for small artichokes and 40 minutes for large artichokes).

Remove artichokes and discard water. Spread each artichoke open very carefully. Reach down into center and remove furry choke, pulling it out a little at a time. Be sure to remove entire choke so you will have a clean, edible artichoke bowl. (The serrated edge of a grapefruit spoon works well for removing entire choke, especially if artichoke is hot.) Serve warm, or chill before serving.

Makes 6 servings

Browned Onions

Each serving contains 71 calories, no cholesterol, 1 g fat, and 4 mg sodium

4 large onions (2 1/2 lb), peeled
1 teaspoon corn oil

I use at least four large onions in this dish, keeping leftovers in the refrigerator to reheat as a garnish on steaks, chops, meat patties, or even chicken.

Slice onions very thinly and set aside. Pour oil into a heavy skillet. With a paper towel wipe oil over entire inner surface of skillet.

Heat skillet over medium heat. Add onions and cook for 30 minutes, stirring frequently. Reduce heat to low and continue cooking onions, stirring occasionally, until they are lightly browned (about another 30 minutes).

Makes 3 cups, six 1/2-cup servings

Asparagus Vinaigrette

Each serving contains 50 calories, no cholesterol, 2 g fat, and 7 mg sodium

30 thin spears asparagus
1 1/2 cups Secret Vinaigrette
   Dressing (see page 46)
1 jar (4 oz) pimientos, drained
   and cut into strips

I often serve this dish as a first course or as a salad, garnishing each asparagus bundle with a strip of pimiento so that it looks as though it is tied with a red ribbon.

Break off and discard tough end of each asparagus stalk by holding stalk in both hands and gently bending stem end until it breaks. Each stalk will break at a slightly different place depending on its toughness. In a large saucepan steam asparagus tips over rapidly boiling water until they are crisp-tender (5 minutes). Remove from heat and immediately place under cold running water. Drain thoroughly, then let cool to room temperature.

In a glass baking dish, place asparagus with all tips pointing in the same direction (to simplify removal). Pour dressing over top, cover dish tightly with plastic wrap, and refrigerate all day or overnight.

To serve, place 5 asparagus tips on each chilled asparagus plate or salad plate and garnish each serving with pimiento strips.

Makes 6 servings

Mushroom Hors d'Oeuvres

Each serving contains 6 calories, no cholesterol, negligible fat, and 1 mg sodium

1 pound large mushrooms
2 cups red wine vinegar, or
   enough to cover mushrooms
1/2 cup Secret Tarragon
   Dressing (see page 45)
1/4 cup minced parsley, for
   garnish

Serve this dish as an hors d'oeuvre with toothpicks for spearing, as a cold vegetable plate in a buffet, or as a garnish for individual salads. When buying fresh mushrooms, make certain to pick those with tightly closed caps, for they are very fresh. Mushrooms with open caps tend to be dry and tough. Allow four hours to marinate and chill the mushrooms.

Wash mushrooms and dry thoroughly. Cut vertically into slices about 1/4 inch thick (4 cups). In a jar or other nonmetallic container, place slices and pour in enough vinegar to cover. Cover container and allow mushrooms to marinate at room temperature for 1 hour.

Pour off and discard vinegar. Remove mushrooms from container and arrange decoratively on a large platter or serving dish. Pour dressing evenly over top, then sprinkle with parsley. Cover platter with plastic wrap and place in the refrigerator for at least 3 hours before serving.

Makes 4 cups, twenty-four 1/8-cup servings

Zucchini in Basil "Butter"

Each serving contains 116 calories, no cholesterol, 9 g fat, and 6 mg sodium

4 medium zucchini (2 lb), sliced
   diagonally
3 tablespoons unsalted corn oil
   margarine
2 teaspoons dried basil, crushed
1/4 teaspoon hot-pepper sauce

This simple and appetizing vegetable side dish can also be combined with fish, poultry, or meat and served as an entrée. I particularly like zucchini with basil, but broccoli, asparagus, or brussels sprouts taste delicious with basil "butter" too.

In a large saucepan steam zucchini over rapidly boiling water until just crisp-tender (3 minutes). Remove from heat and immediately place under cold running water. Drain thoroughly.

In a large skillet over medium heat, melt margarine; add basil and hot-pepper sauce and stir to blend. Place steamed zucchini in basil mixture and heat until warm. Serve immediately.

Makes 4 cups, four 1-cup servings

Marinated Zucchini Spears

Each serving contains 92 calories, no cholesterol, 5 g fat, and 8 mg sodium

6 medium zucchini (3 lb), cut lengthwise into quarters

¹/₄ cup freshly squeezed lemon juice

1¹/₂ cups Secret Cumin Dressing (see page 45)

1 large ripe tomato, peeled and diced (1 cup)

1 medium onion, peeled and diced (1¹/₂ cups)

1 cup finely minced parsley, for garnish

With its festive colors this dish is perfect for holiday menus. Serve the zucchini spears as an appetizer, a salad, or a cold vegetable side dish. Be sure to allow four hours to marinate and chill the zucchini.

In a glass baking dish place zucchini quarters and pour lemon juice evenly over top. Cover and allow to stand for at least 1 hour.

Pour off and discard liquid. In a large saucepan steam zucchini over rapidly boiling water until just crisp-tender (3 minutes). Transfer zucchini back to baking dish, pour dressing over top, and allow zucchini to cool to room temperature.

Scatter tomato and onion over zucchini, cover, and chill for at least 3 hours before serving.

To serve, divide zucchini evenly among 8 chilled plates and sprinkle with parsley.

Makes 10 cups, eight 1¹/₄-cup servings

Chinese Snow Peas and Water Chestnuts

Each serving contains 68 calories, no cholesterol, 3 g fat, and 5 mg sodium

2 teaspoons each corn oil and dark sesame oil

2 teaspoons grated fresh ginger or ¹/₄ teaspoon ground ginger

³/₄ pound snow peas (4¹/₂ cups), strings removed and ends notched

¹/₄ cup dry sherry

2 teaspoons freshly squeezed lemon juice

1 can (6 oz) water chestnuts, drained and very thinly sliced

This is an attractive, interestingly crunchy accompaniment to Asian dishes, such as Cantonese Sweet-and-Sour Pork (see page 116). Refrigerated leftovers can be added to a salad. For a fancy presentation I like to cut the ends of the pea pods in a V shape.

In a large skillet or wok over low heat, warm oils. Add ginger and stir a few seconds. Add peas and cook, stirring constantly, until crisp-tender (about 5 minutes).

Add sherry, lemon juice, and water chestnuts; cook for 2 more minutes, stirring constantly. Serve immediately.

Makes 4 cups, eight ¹/₂-cup servings

Curried Zucchini Purée

Each serving contains 45 calories, negligible cholesterol, 1 g fat, and 15 mg sodium

½ cup water

1 teaspoon sugar

4 small zucchini (1½ lb), sliced (6 cups)

1 medium onion, peeled and chopped (1½ cups)

1 cup nonfat milk

2 teaspoons unsalted corn oil margarine

1 tablespoon flour

1 teaspoon curry powder

¼ teaspoon ground ginger

2 teaspoons freshly squeezed lemon juice

Puréed vegetables are an occasional treat, and this recipe is always well received. If you have any left over, chill it and use it as a low-calorie dip for other cold, raw, or cooked vegetables.

In a large saucepan over high heat, combine the water and sugar and bring to a boil. Add zucchini and onion, cover, reduce heat to low, and simmer until just tender (about 5 minutes). Transfer mixture with liquid, to a blender container and blend until smooth; set aside.

In a small saucepan over low heat, simmer milk. In a large saucepan over medium heat, melt margarine. Add flour to margarine and cook for 3 minutes, stirring constantly. Do not brown. Remove pan from heat and add milk all at once, stirring constantly with a wire whisk. Add curry powder and ginger and mix well.

Place pan over low heat and cook for 20 minutes, stirring occasionally. Remove from heat; add lemon juice and zucchini mixture and mix well. Return to low heat and warm to desired temperature before serving.

Makes about 5 cups, ten ½-cup servings

Baked Parsley

Each serving contains 32 calories, no cholesterol, no fat, and 24 mg sodium

1 large bunch parsley, coarsely
  chopped (4 cups)
2 quarts water
1 tablespoon sugar

Eating this delightfully different vegetable dish is like eating cotton candy: When you start to chew, the mouthful disappears as if by magic. Baked Parsley is also a lovely low-calorie topping for other vegetables and for soups, salads, fish, poultry, and meats. Soaking the parsley in sugared water before baking adds flavor.

In a large container combine parsley, the water, and sugar; let stand for 1 hour.

Preheat oven to 350° F. Thoroughly drain parsley and spread it evenly in a large baking dish. Bake until parsley is crisp (about 25 minutes).

Makes 2 cups, four ¹/₂-cup servings

Savory Tomatoes Au Gratin

Each serving contains 47 calories, 6 mg cholesterol, 2 g fat, and 40 mg sodium

4 large ripe tomatoes (1¹/₂ lb)
¹/₂ cup nonfat milk
1 teaspoon freshly squeezed
  lemon juice
2 teaspoons dried summer
  savory, crushed
¹/₂ cup grated low-sodium
  Cheddar cheese

This dish is an excellent accompaniment to fish, poultry, and meat entrées and to omelets for brunch. If you wish, add more cheese and make it a picture-perfect vegetarian entrée.

Preheat oven to 400° F. Cut tomatoes in half, remove and discard seeds, and place tomato halves, cut side up, in a shallow flameproof dish. Combine milk and lemon juice; drizzle 1 tablespoon of the mixture onto each tomato half. Sprinkle ¹/₄ teaspoon summer savory over each tomato half; top with 1 tablespoon grated cheese.

Bake tomatoes for 15 minutes, then place under the broiler until they are lightly browned.

Makes 8 half-tomato servings

Open-Faced BLT
Each serving contains 245 calories, 17 mg cholesterol, 17 g fat, and 21 mg sodium

¼ cup Unsalted Mayonnaise (see page 37)
¼ teaspoon smoke flavoring
4 slices Low-Sodium Whole Wheat Bread (see page 122), toasted
2 medium ripe tomatoes, thinly sliced
Freshly ground black pepper, for sprinkling
4 large lettuce leaves
Parsley sprigs, for garnish

Serve this bacon-flavored version of the classic bacon, lettuce, and tomato sandwich to your salt-loving friends and amaze them with the taste. I like to serve bite-sized BLTs for cocktail parties and teas, making each sandwich small enough to be indeed one bite; otherwise, they are messy to eat at stand-up, no-plate functions.

In a small bowl combine mayonnaise and smoke flavoring and mix well. Spread 1 tablespoon of the mayonnaise mixture evenly on each slice of toast. Arrange all but 4 tomato slices evenly on top. Sprinkle each sandwich lightly with pepper, then place a lettuce leaf and 1 reserved tomato slice on top of each. Place each sandwich on a plate, garnish with parsley, and serve.

Makes 4 open-faced sandwiches

Baked Spaghetti Squash
Each serving contains 46 calories, no cholesterol, negligible fat, and 28 mg sodium

1 medium spaghetti squash (5 lb)

Although cooked spaghetti squash looks like spaghetti, it has only about one fourth the calories. You can use spaghetti squash for making Vegetarian Spaghetti (see page 69) or serve it with just a touch of extra virgin olive oil and a light sprinkling of freshly grated Parmesan cheese.

Preheat oven to 350° F. Cut squash in half with a heavy knife, and remove and discard seeds. (Cutting the squash lengthwise gives longer strands.) In a baking dish place halves, cut side down, and bake until fork-tender (about 1 hour).

Remove squash from oven; with a fork pull strands of cooked flesh from skin. Serve immediately.

Makes 8 cups, eight 1-cup servings

Vegetarian Spaghetti

Each serving contains 339 calories, 2 mg cholesterol, 5 g fat, and 100 mg sodium

4 quarts water
2 cloves garlic, minced
1 teaspoon freshly squeezed lemon juice
1 tablespoon extra virgin olive oil
1 pound spaghetti
6 cups Marinara Sauce (see page 32), heated to serving temperature
1/4 cup freshly grated Parmesan cheese
1/4 cup low-sodium bread crumbs, toasted (see page 119)

For an all-vegetable spaghetti dish, substitute 6 cups Baked Spaghetti Squash (see page 68) for the spaghetti. Serve this dish with garlic bread and a green salad with Secret Italian Dressing (see page 46).

In a large saucepan or stockpot over high heat, bring the water to a boil. Add garlic, lemon juice, and oil and boil for 5 minutes. Add spaghetti and cook until it is al dente (8 to 10 minutes). Drain well and toss with sauce. Divide among eight warm dinner plates.

Combine cheese and bread crumbs and mix well. Sprinkle 1 tablespoon of the mixture over each serving.

Makes 12 cups, eight 1½-cup servings

Vegetarian Casserole

Each serving contains 133 calories, 68 mg cholesterol, 6 g fat, and 25 mg sodium

1/2 cup finely chopped almonds
2 eggs, slightly beaten
1 teaspoon dried marjoram, crushed
1/2 teaspoon dried sage, crushed
1/2 teaspoon dried thyme, crushed
1 medium eggplant (1 lb), unpeeled, diced (6 cups)
2 medium onions, peeled and finely chopped (3 cups)
2 large red apples, unpeeled, cored and diced (3 cups)
1 cup finely chopped parsley

This tempting eggplant casserole is an interesting variation on traditional stuffings made with bread or rice. Serve it with turkey for a holiday menu or with other poultry, fish, or meat anytime during the year.

Preheat oven to 350° F. Toast almonds on a baking sheet until they are golden brown (8 to 10 minutes). Watch carefully, since they burn easily. Set aside.

In a large mixing bowl, combine eggs, marjoram, sage, and thyme; mix thoroughly. Add eggplant, onions, apples, and parsley, and again mix well. Place in a casserole, cover, and bake for 1 hour.

Just before serving, either stir in the toasted almonds or sprinkle them over each serving.

Makes 8 cups, eight 1-cup servings

Caraway Cabbage

Each serving contains 61 calories, no cholesterol, 3 g fat, and 27 mg sodium

2 tablespoons unsalted corn oil margarine
1 large head white cabbage (2 ½ lb), finely shredded (12 cups)
1½ teaspoons caraway seed

Many people who think they do not like cabbage will rave about this dish. Try it with Mustard Sauce (see page 32). It is good served hot, cold, or (my favorite) at room temperature.

In a large skillet over medium heat, melt margarine. Add cabbage and cook, stirring until crisp-tender (8 to 10 minutes). Remove from heat, add caraway seeds, and mix thoroughly. Serve immediately, let cool to room temperature, or refrigerate and serve cold.

Makes 8 cups, eight 1-cup servings

Italian Eggplant

Each serving contains 105 calories, 10 mg cholesterol, 5 g fat, and 59 mg sodium

2 cups unsalted tomato juice
2 tablespoons red wine vinegar
1 medium onion, peeled and finely chopped (1½ cups)
1½ teaspoons dried oregano, crushed
1 tablespoon extra virgin olive oil
Freshly ground black pepper, for sprinkling
1 large firm eggplant (1½ lb), unpeeled, cut crosswise into ¼-inch-thick slices
¼ pound low-sodium Monterey jack cheese, grated (1 cup)

Surprise dinner guests with this delicious low-calorie taste treat. It is a wonderful dish for entertaining because it can be prepared in advance and baked right before serving.

In a large saucepan over medium heat, combine tomato juice, vinegar, and onion. Bring to a boil, reduce heat to low, and simmer, uncovered, for 45 minutes. Add oregano and simmer for another 30 minutes. Set aside.

Preheat oven to 400° F. In a large skillet over medium-high heat, warm 1½ teaspoons of the oil. Sprinkle pepper on eggplant slices. Sauté half the slices in hot oil until they are fork-tender and golden brown on both sides. Repeat with remaining oil and eggplant

Place cooked eggplant in a large baking dish. Spread tomato mixture evenly over eggplant and bake for 10 minutes.

Remove baking dish from oven and sprinkle grated cheese evenly over eggplant. Place dish under the broiler until cheese is melted and lightly browned. Serve hot.

Makes 8 servings

Eggplant Sublime

Each serving contains 115 calories, no cholesterol, 4 g fat, and 22 mg sodium

2 medium eggplants, unpeeled
(1 lb each)
2 tablespoons corn oil
2 cans (16 oz each) unsalted
stewed tomatoes, undrained
1 cup water
$1/2$ cup red wine vinegar
1 teaspoon ground coriander
1 teaspoon dried sage, crushed
$1/2$ teaspoon dried thyme,
crushed
$1/2$ teaspoon dried rosemary,
crushed
$1/2$ teaspoon cracked black
pepper
2 large cloves garlic, pressed
$1/2$ lemon, sliced
1 large green bell pepper, seeded
and thinly sliced (2 cups)
1 medium onion, peeled and
thinly sliced (2 cups)
1 tablespoon sugar

Like Vegetarian Casserole (see page 69), this savory eggplant dish can accompany fish, poultry, or meat. It can also stand on its own as a vegetarian entrée; just sprinkle the top with a low-sodium cheese of your choice right before serving.

Trim stems from eggplants and cut eggplants crosswise into $1/4$-inch-thick slices. In a large, heavy skillet over medium-high heat, warm 2 teaspoons of the oil. Sauté one third of the eggplant slices until lightly browned on both sides; set aside. Repeat with remaining eggplant and oil.

Preheat oven to 350° F. In a large saucepan over medium heat, combine remaining ingredients. Bring to a boil, reduce heat to low, and simmer, uncovered, until amount is reduced by half (about 2 hours).

Arrange 1 layer of eggplant in a casserole dish, then top with some of the sauce. Repeat with remaining eggplant and sauce. Cover dish and bake for 1 hour.

Makes 4 cups, eight $1/2$-cup servings

Portuguese Pilaf

Each serving contains 185 calories, no cholesterol, 4 g fat, and 8 mg sodium

2 tablespoons corn oil
2 cloves garlic, minced
1 1/2 cups uncooked long-grain
    brown rice
1 medium onion, peeled and
    thinly sliced (2 cups)
2 cups Unsalted Chicken Stock
    (see page 17), boiling
1 teaspoon dried oregano,
    crushed
1/2 teaspoon each chili powder
    and ground cumin
1/4 teaspoon freshly ground black
    pepper
1/8 teaspoon hot-pepper sauce

Even better when made a day in advance, this pilaf can be reheated by adding a little stock or water, cover and heat at 300° F oven for about 30 minutes.

Preheat oven to 400° F. In a heavy skillet over medium heat, warm oil. Add garlic, rice, and onion; cook until browned, stirring frequently (about 5 minutes). Transfer rice mixture to a casserole dish with a tight-fitting lid.

    Combine remaining ingredients with stock, add to rice mixture, and stir to blend. Cover and bake for 40 minutes. Allow to stand, covered, for 10 minutes before serving.

Makes 4 cups, eight 1/2 cup servings

Baked Beans

Each serving contains 221 calories, no cholesterol, 1 g fat, and 21 mg sodium

1 pound dried pinto beans
    (2 1/2 cups)
6 cups water
2 medium onions, peeled and
    finely chopped (3 cups)
4 cloves garlic, minced
2 bay leaves
1 can (16 oz) unsalted stewed
    tomatoes, undrained
1/2 cup sugar
1 tablespoon chili powder
1 teaspoon ground mustard
1 teaspoon dried oregano,
    crushed
1 tablespoon smoke flavoring
1/4 cup red wine vinegar

If you like baked beans, you will love this version. It is practical from every standpoint: It is easy and inexpensive to prepare, and it keeps for days in the refrigerator. Served with plain brown rice, it makes a complete protein for a delicious vegetarian lunch or dinner.

In a large saucepan soak beans overnight in the water. Discard any beans that have floated to the top. Add onions, garlic, and bay leaves and bring to a boil over medium-high heat. Lower heat, cover, and simmer until beans are tender (about 1 1/2 hours)

    Preheat oven to 350° F. In a 7- by 12-inch baking dish, combine beans with remaining ingredients. Bake until liquid is absorbed (about 1 hour).

Makes 7 1/2 cups, ten 3/4-cup servings

Wild Rice à l'Orange

Each serving contains 166 calories, no cholesterol, 8 g fat, and 5 mg sodium

3/4 cup uncooked wild rice
2 cups Unsalted Chicken Stock
*   (see page 17)*
2 tablespoons freshly grated
*   orange zest*
1 teaspoon dried thyme, crushed
1/2 cup chopped almonds
1 tablespoon unsalted corn oil
*   margarine*

This tangy wild rice can be served cold, at room temperature, or hot. When serving it as a salad, I eliminate the margarine and sprinkle it with the toasted almonds. A favorite salad is room-temperature wild rice topped with warm grilled chicken breasts. Cold wild rice tossed with leftover cooked turkey is also good.

In a medium saucepan over medium heat, combine rice, stock, orange zest, and thyme. Bring to a boil, reduce heat to low, cover, and simmer until all liquid is absorbed and rice is fluffy (55 to 65 minutes). Remove from heat and set aside.

Preheat oven to 350° F. Toast almonds on a baking sheet until they are golden brown (8 to 10 minutes). Watch carefully; they burn easily. Combine cooked rice, toasted almonds, and margarine and mix thoroughly. Serve hot.

Makes 4 cups, eight 1/2-cup servings

Southern Yam Casserole

Each serving contains 92 calories, negligible cholesterol, no fat, and 53 mg sodium

2 medium yams, cooked,
*   peeled, and mashed (2 cups)*
3/4 cup nonfat milk
1/2 cup freshly squeezed orange
*   juice*
1 tablespoon freshly grated
*   orange zest*
1/2 teaspoon freshly grated
*   nutmeg*
1/4 cup sugar
6 egg whites, beaten until firm
*   but not dry*
Nonstick vegetable coating, to
*   spray dish*

When grating the orange peel for this casserole, be careful to use only the orange part of the rind, known as the zest. The white part will make the dish bitter. Also, use freshly grated nutmeg if possible. It has a stronger flavor than the ground nutmeg found in jars and cans.

Preheat oven to 350° F. In a large bowl combine yams, milk, orange juice, orange zest, nutmeg, and sugar; mix well. Fold in egg whites.

Spray a casserole dish with nonstick vegetable coating. Pour mixture into dish and bake, uncovered, for 45 minutes. Serve hot.

Makes 4 cups, eight 1/2-cup servings

B & B Potato Boats

Each serving contains 227 calories, 1 mg cholesterol, 4 g fat, and 37 mg sodium

3 *large baking potatoes (2 lb)*
Corn oil, for rubbing potatoes
1 *medium onion, peeled and
    thinly sliced (2 cups)*
2 *tablespoons unsalted corn oil
    margarine*
$1/3$ *cup nonfat milk*
$1/4$ *teaspoon ground white
    pepper*
$1/2$ *teaspoon onion powder*
$1/2$ *teaspoon smoke flavoring*
1 *tablespoon freshly grated
    Parmesan cheese*
Paprika, for sprinkling

These baked and broiled potato "boats" are a satisfying addition to a summer patio barbecue. Reheated and wrapped, they can also be taken to beach parties and picnics.

Preheat oven to 400° F. Thoroughly scrub potatoes so that skins are clean enough to eat. Rub skin of each potato with oil, then cut potato in half lengthwise. Divide onion evenly among potato halves. Reassemble potatoes to enclose onion, then wrap each tightly with aluminum foil. Arrange wrapped potatoes in a baking dish or on a cookie sheet, place in the center of the oven, and bake for 1 hour.

Remove potatoes from oven and unwrap. Transfer cooked onion to a large mixing bowl. Carefully scoop potato meat from each potato half without tearing skin; add potato meat to cooked onion. Reserve potato skins to use as "boats." Add margarine to potato-onion mixture. In a small bowl combine milk, pepper, onion powder, and smoke flavoring; stir well and add to mixture.

With an electric mixer or potato masher, whip mixture until thoroughly blended and smooth in texture. Divide mixture evenly among potato skins. Sprinkle $1/2$ teaspoon cheese on top of each, then a little paprika. Place potato boats under the broiler until they are lightly browned.

Makes 6 half-potato servings

EGGS, EGG SUBSTITUTE, AND CHEESE

Egg substitutes and low-sodium cheeses have increased the variety of dishes available to those watching their salt intake. Be aware, however, that most egg substitutes are higher in sodium than eggs. My recipe for Egg Substitute on page 76 has negligible cholesterol (compared to 213 milligrams in a large egg), it is lower in sodium than both commercial egg substitutes and eggs, and it contains no artificial coloring or preservatives.

The sodium figure given with each recipe is based on 63 milligrams of sodium per large egg and on the average number of milligrams per ounce for most low-sodium cheeses. Excellent cheeses whose fat content is reduced 20 percent are also available; they are lower in sodium and cholesterol than regular cheeses and can be substituted in recipes calling for regular cheeses without any appreciable difference in taste. Cheeses with a fat reduction greater than 20 percent tend to become rubbery when cooked.

Commercial cottage cheese is also high in sodium, and low-sodium cottage cheese can be difficult to find. I suggest using low-fat cottage cheese, putting it in a strainer or some cheesecloth, and holding it under cold running water; rinsing eliminates most of the sodium. Ricotta cheese may be handled the same way. Dry-curd cottage cheese, or hoop cheese, can be substituted for cottage cheese in many recipes. It is very low in both sodium and fat.

Egg Substitute

Each serving contains 62 calories, negligible cholesterol, 5 g fat, and 58 mg sodium

2 egg whites (see page 164)
2 teaspoons corn oil
2 teaspoons instant nonfat dry
milk powder

This egg substitute is easy to make and much less expensive than commercial egg substitutes. It can replace whole eggs in recipes, including recipes for omelets, soufflés, quiches, and scrambled eggs. It lacks the yellow egg-yolk color of commercial brands because it does not contain artificial coloring, but for most recipes color does not present a problem. You can multiply this recipe, which makes ¹/₂ cup—the equivalent of two eggs—by any amount. Egg Substitute will keep for about two days.

Combine all ingredients and mix well. Refrigerate.

Makes about ¹/₂ cup, two ¹/₄-cup servings

Poached Eggs

Each serving contains 75 calories, 213 mg cholesterol, 5 g fat, and 63 mg sodium

2 quarts water
2 tablespoons distilled white
vinegar
1 tablespoon freshly squeezed
lemon juice
Eggs, as many as desired

You can make these eggs ahead of time and store them in the refrigerator in a bowl of ice water. To reheat the eggs, place them in a large sauce pan of warm water and bring the water almost to a boil. Remove the eggs and blot them with a paper towel before serving.

In a large sauce pan over high heat, combine the water, vinegar, and lemon juice and bring to a boil.

Break each egg into a saucer, one at a time, and slide it into the boiling water, working quickly so that eggs cook evenly. Reduce heat to a simmer and poach eggs to desired firmness (2 to 3 minutes). Do not cook too many eggs at once, since they will be difficult to handle.

Remove eggs from water with a slotted spoon and dip each egg into a bowl of warm water to rinse it. Blot with a paper towel before serving.

Each serving is 1 egg

Basic Omelet

Each serving contains 169 calories, 426 mg cholesterol, 12 g fat, and 127 mg sodium

2 eggs
Dash ground white pepper
Dash freshly ground black
  pepper
2 teaspoons water
1 teaspoon freshly squeezed
  lemon juice
$^1/_2$ teaspoon unsalted corn oil
  margarine

You can fill an omelet with any ingredient you want such as leftover cooked vegetables, cold fish, poultry, or meat, a sauce, or even a fruit dessert. Whatever you use should be at hand when you pour the beaten egg into the pan. Then, before folding the omelet, arrange the filling in a strip down the center and fold the omelet as directed. Calculate the caloric and sodium content using the guide on page 170. Omelets made with leftovers are my favorite Sunday brunch entrée. My children call them clean-the-refrigerator specials, since each person's omelet often contains a different leftover.

In a small bowl beat eggs with a fork or wire whisk until they are frothy. Add white and black peppers, the water, and lemon juice; beat again.

In a 10-inch omelet pan or skillet over high heat, melt margarine until it is very hot. Reduce heat to medium and pour in egg mixture. Tilt pan so that mixture coats most of its inner surface. Use a fork to lift edges of omelet, tilting pan so some mixture from the center runs underneath edges to cook.

When the bottom of the omelet is cooked and the top is still a bit runny, fold edges toward the center. Slide omelet onto a plate and serve.

Makes 1 serving

Cheese and Chive Omelet

Each serving contains 228 calories, 233 mg cholesterol, 15 g fat, and 173 mg sodium

1 egg
2 egg whites
Dash ground white pepper
1/2 teaspoon smoke flavoring
1 tablespoon water
1/4 cup chopped chives
1/2 teaspoon unsalted corn oil
   margarine
1/4 cup grated low-sodium
   cheese of your choice

All Dr. Seuss fans who love green eggs and ham should love this dish. While ham is too high in sodium to be included in this recipe, the eggs are indeed green!

In a blender container place egg, egg whites, pepper, smoke flavoring, the water, and chives and blend until frothy.

In a 10-inch omelet pan or skillet over high heat, melt margarine until it is very hot. Reduce heat to medium and pour in beaten egg mixture. Tilt pan so that mixture coats most of its inner surface. Use a fork to lift edges of omelet, tilting pan so some mixture from the center runs underneath edges to cook.

When the bottom of the omelet is cooked and the top is still a bit runny, sprinkle cheese in a strip down the center. Then fold edges toward the center. Slide omelet onto a plate and serve.

Makes 1 serving

Eggs Benedict

Each serving contains 300 calories, 300 mg cholesterol, 19 g fat, and 116 mg sodium

2 teaspoons unsalted corn oil
   margarine
1/4 teaspoon smoke flavoring
4 thin slices (1 oz each) cooked
   turkey breast meat
3/4 cup Sauce Hollandaise Sans
   Sel (see page 35)
2 Low-Sodium English
   Muffins, split and toasted
   (see page 124)
4 Poached Eggs (see page 76)
Paprika, for sprinkling
   (optional)

This dish is a fabulous fake. The smoke flavoring makes the turkey slices taste very much like the traditionally used Canadian bacon, which is high in sodium. Serve as a brunch entrée for friends on low-sodium diets—they will love you for it!

In a large skillet over medium heat, melt margarine. Add smoke flavoring and mix thoroughly. Arrange turkey slices in skillet and heat, turning frequently, until they are lightly browned on both sides.

Spread 1 tablespoon hollandaise sauce on each toasted muffin half. Place a browned turkey slice on top of each, then place a poached egg on top of each turkey slice. Spoon 2 tablespoons hollandaise sauce on top of each serving, and sprinkle with paprika (if desired).

Makes 4 servings

Peaches 'n' Cream Omelet

Each serving contains 311 calories, 449 mg cholesterol, 19 g fat, and 151 mg sodium

¹/₄ cup light sour cream
2 teaspoons sugar
¹/₄ teaspoon vanilla extract
2 eggs
2 teaspoons water
1 teaspoon freshly squeezed lemon juice
¹/₂ teaspoon unsalted corn oil margarine
1 small peach, peeled and diced (¹/₂ cup)
Ground cinnamon, for sprinkling

You can substitute other fresh fruit or berries in season for the peaches in this omelet or use canned peaches packed either in water or natural juice without added sugar or salt. If you serve this omelet for dessert, halve the serving size.

In a small bowl combine sour cream, 1 teaspoon of the sugar, and vanilla. Mix well; set aside.

In a medium bowl beat eggs with a fork or wire whisk until they are frothy. Add remaining sugar, the water, and lemon juice; beat again.

In a 10-inch omelet pan or skillet over high heat, melt margarine until it is very hot. Reduce heat to medium and pour in egg mixture. Tilt pan so that mixture coats most of its inner surface. Use a fork to lift edges of omelet, tilting pan so some mixture from the center runs underneath edges to cook.

When the bottom of the omelet is cooked and the top is still a bit runny, spoon diced peach in a strip down the center. Then fold edges toward the center and slide omelet onto a plate. Spoon sour cream mixture over top and sprinkle with a little cinnamon.

Makes 1 serving

Soufflé sans Sel

Each serving contains 142 calories, 82 mg cholesterol, 8 g fat, and 105 mg sodium

1   cup nonfat milk
2   tablespoons unsalted corn oil
    margarine
1/2   cup minced onion
2 1/2   tablespoons flour
2   egg yolks
1   teaspoon freshly squeezed
    lemon juice
1/8   teaspoon ground white
    pepper
Dash hot-pepper sauce
2   ounces low-sodium Cheddar
    cheese, grated (1/2 cup)
1/4   teaspoon cream of tartar
6   egg whites, at room
    temperature

You can make this soufflé mixture many hours before you plan to serve it, but once it goes in the oven, remember the old saying "You must wait for a soufflé because it won't wait for you." It will fall very quickly after being removed from the oven, so plan the timing of the rest of the meal around this dish.

Preheat oven to 400° F. In a small saucepan over low heat, bring milk to a simmer.

In a large saucepan over medium heat, melt margarine; add onion and cook until onion is soft and translucent, stirring frequently. Add flour and cook for 3 minutes, stirring constantly. Do not brown.

Remove flour mixture from heat and pour in simmering milk all at once, stirring with a wire whisk. Return pan to medium heat and allow mixture to come to a boil, stirring constantly. Boil for 1 minute; sauce will be quite thick. Remove from heat and add egg yolks, one at a time, stirring each one in thoroughly with a wire whisk. Mix in lemon juice, pepper, and hot-pepper sauce.

If soufflé was prepared ahead of time, reheat mixture in a covered saucepan until it is lukewarm. Add cheese and mix well. In a large bowl add cream of tartar to egg whites and beat until stiff but not dry. Stir one fourth of egg-white mixture into cheese mixture to lighten soufflé base. Fold in remaining egg-white mixture, being careful not to overmix.

Pour mixture into an 8-inch-diameter soufflé dish. Place dish in the center of the oven. Immediately reduce heat to 375° F and cook until soufflé is set and golden brown (20 to 25 minutes). Serve immediately.

Makes 4 cups, six 2/3-cup servings

Cottage Cheese Crêpes

Each serving contains 123 calories, 10 mg cholesterol, 3 g fat, and 162 mg sodium

2 cups low-fat cottage cheese, rinsed (see page 75)
1/4 cup grated low-sodium Monterey jack cheese
2 tablespoons grated onion
1 tablespoon finely chopped parsley
1 tablespoon finely chopped chives
1 clove garlic, minced
6 Low-Sodium Crêpes, warmed (see page 134)
2 tablespoons freshly grated Parmesan cheese

Crêpes, instead of bread, can accompany an all-vegetable salad. Rinsing the cottage cheese before using it greatly reduces the sodium in this recipe.

Preheat oven to 350° F. In a large mixing bowl, combine cottage cheese, jack cheese, onion, parsley, chives, and garlic. Mix thoroughly.

Place crêpes on a clean work surface and spoon cheese mixture evenly down the center of each, using 6 to 7 tablespoons per crêpe. Fold crêpe over filling and place each crêpe, seam side down, in a glass baking dish. Sprinkle Parmesan cheese over top of crêpes and bake until Parmesan cheese is lightly browned (about 20 minutes).

Makes six 1-crêpe servings

Lemon French Toast

Each serving contains 154 calories, 71 mg cholesterol, 3 g fat, and 71 mg sodium

1/2 cup nonfat milk
1/2 teaspoon freshly squeezed lemon juice
2 eggs, beaten
4 egg whites, beaten
6 slices Low-Sodium French Bread (see page 120)
1 tablespoon unsalted corn oil margarine

The lemon juice in this recipe substitutes amazingly well for salt. You may enjoy serving this new French toast with just a sprinkling of powdered sugar, additional freshly squeezed lemon juice, and a garnish of lemon slices, although it is also good with Honey "Butter" (see page 41), fresh fruit, or Strawberry Jelly (see page 157).

In a shallow dish combine milk and lemon juice; mix well. Add eggs and egg whites; beat until they are frothy. Dip each slice of bread into mixture, turning it over to soak up liquid.

In a large skillet over medium-high heat, melt margarine. Cook egg-soaked bread until it is lightly browned on both sides. Serve with your choice of accompaniments.

Makes 6 servings

Huevos Rancheros

Each serving contains 317 calories, 243 mg cholesterol, 17 g fat, and 139 mg sodium

1 tablespoon corn oil

1 medium onion, peeled and finely chopped (1½ cups)

1 medium green bell pepper, seeded and finely chopped (⅔ cup)

3 cloves garlic, minced

2 cans (16 oz each) unsalted stewed tomatoes

2 large green chiles, seeded, deveined, and chopped (⅔ cup)

½ teaspoon freshly ground black pepper

2 teaspoons chili powder

2 teaspoons dried oregano, crushed

½ teaspoon ground cumin

6 eggs, at room temperature

6 ounces low-sodium Cheddar cheese, grated (1½ cups)

6 corn tortillas, warmed

This sensational southwestern breakfast dish is my addition to the menus at the Canyon Ranch spas. However, these spas use egg whites alone, instead of whole eggs, to lower the cholesterol.

In a large skillet over medium heat, warm oil. Add onion, bell pepper, and garlic; cook until onion is translucent. Add tomatoes, chiles, ground pepper, chili powder, oregano, and cumin; cook, uncovered, for 20 minutes.

Make 6 small depressions in the sauce with the back of a spoon and carefully break an egg into each depression. Sprinkle cheese over all, then cover and cook until egg whites are opaque and cheese is melted (3 to 5 minutes). Serve each egg on top of a warm tortilla. Spoon some of the sauce remaining in pan over each serving.

Makes 6 servings

Matzo Balls Au Gratin

Each serving contains 258 calories, 70 mg cholesterol, 13 g fat, and 118 mg sodium

2 cups nonfat milk
1 tablespoon unsalted corn oil margarine
3 tablespoons flour
1/4 teaspoon ground white pepper
1/2 teaspoon ground mustard
1/2 cup grated low-sodium Cheddar cheese
12 Low-Sodium Matzo Balls (see page 137)

Several years ago I created this recipe for the feast that breaks the fast of Yom Kippur. Several Jewish friends who keep kosher kitchens and who, therefore, do not serve meat and dairy dishes on the same plate or even at the same time were invited. I decided it would be fun to serve matzo balls with cheese as an appetizer rather than serve them in the traditional chicken soup.

In a small saucepan over low heat, bring milk to a simmer. In a medium saucepan over medium heat, melt margarine. Add flour to margarine and cook 3 minutes, stirring constantly. Do not brown. Remove from heat and add simmering milk all at once, stirring constantly with a wire whisk. Add pepper, mustard, and cheese; mix well. Return sauce to low heat and cook slowly for 30 minutes, stirring occasionally.

Preheat oven to 350° F. Arrange matzo balls in a flat baking dish or 4 individual au gratin dishes; pour warm cheese sauce over top. Bake until cheese is lightly browned (about 30 minutes), or bake for 20 minutes and then place dish under the broiler to lightly brown cheese sauce before serving.

Makes 4 servings

FISH AND SHELLFISH

Fish is the best source of animal protein because it contains less fat than either poultry or meat. Fresh fish is also the leading source of omega-3 fatty acids, which are believed to reduce the risk of coronary artery disease.

If you think you do not like fish, chances are you have eaten overcooked fish, which is dry and tasteless, or never eaten really fresh fish. When buying a whole fresh fish, look for very clear eyes and scales that lie flat against the skin. Filleted fresh fish should look moist, not dry. No fresh fish or shellfish should have an overly strong "fishy" smell. If fresh fish is not available, buy fresh-frozen fish and before cooking it let it thaw slowly in the refrigerator, or under cold running water if you are in a hurry. To store fish and also to avoid the fishy taste that many people find objectionable, wash the fish with cold water and pat it dry. Cover the fish with freshly squeezed lemon juice and store, tightly covered, in a nonaluminum container in the refrigerator for at least two hours before cooking it. The lemon juice marinade also reduces the need for salt in its preparation.

When cooking fish the single most important thing to remember is not to overcook it. The minute it turns from translucent to opaque, it is done. Further cooking will only lessen the flavor and make the fish tough and dry.

Shellfish tends to be higher in sodium than other fish and therefore must be used sparingly in a low-sodium diet. Canned fish and shellfish should be rinsed thoroughly with cold running water to eliminate as much of the sodium as possible before using the fish in your recipes.

Fillet of Sole with Walnuts

Each serving contains 204 calories, 55 mg cholesterol, 12 g fat, and 95 mg sodium

8 small sole fillets (2 lb)
2 lemons
$^1/_2$ cup finely chopped walnuts
4 tablespoons unsalted corn oil
   margarine

Fillet of sole with almonds, or sole amandine, is the traditional recipe for sole. I think the delicate flavor of sole is enhanced by walnuts. Try my recipe and see if you agree.

Wash fish in cold water and pat dry. Place fish in a flat glass baking dish and squeeze juice of 1 lemon evenly over top. Turn fish over and squeeze on juice of remaining lemon. Cover and refrigerate for at least 2 hours.

Preheat oven to 350° F. Toast walnuts on a baking sheet until they are golden brown (8 to 10 minutes). Watch carefully; they burn easily. Set aside.

In a large skillet over medium heat, melt 2 tablespoons of the margarine. Add $^1/_4$ cup of the toasted walnuts. Place fish in skillet with walnuts and sauté on both sides until fish turns from translucent to opaque (about 8 minutes). Do not overcook. Remove fish from skillet and place on warmed individual plates or on a serving platter.

Melt remaining margarine in the same skillet and mix in remaining toasted walnuts. Spoon walnut mixture over cooked fish and serve.

Makes 8 servings

Fish Fillets à la Véronique

Each serving contains 163 calories, 63 mg cholesterol, 2 g fat, and 100 mg sodium

2 pounds firm white fish fillets,
  preferably sea bass or red
  snapper
2 lemons
Ground white pepper, for
  sprinkling
1/4 cup dry white wine
2 cups seedless grapes
2 tablespoons arrowroot
1 tablespoon sugar
2 tablespoons water
1/2 teaspoon dried tarragon,
  crushed
2/3 cup Unsalted White Sauce
  (see page 33), heated to
  serving temperature

This beautiful dish is garnished with small bunches of seedless grapes. I like to serve it with a combination of colorful seasonal vegetables and Dill Bread (see page 126).

Wash fish in cold water and pat dry. Place fish in a flat glass baking dish, squeeze juice of 1 lemon over top, and sprinkle with pepper. Turn fish over and squeeze on juice of remaining lemon and again lightly sprinkle with pepper. Cover dish tightly with aluminum foil or a lid and refrigerate for at least 2 hours.

Preheat oven to 350° F. Remove cover from dish and pour wine over fish. Reseal dish and bake fish until it turns from translucent to opaque (about 20 minutes). Remove from oven and place fish on warmed plates or a serving platter; keep warm.

Pour liquid in which fish was cooked into a saucepan, add grapes, and bring mixture to a boil, cooking just until grapes begin to split. In a small bowl combine arrowroot, sugar, and the water and mix well. Add arrowroot mixture and tarragon to grape sauce and cook until thickened, stirring constantly. Remove from heat; add white sauce; mix thoroughly. Pour sauce over fish and serve.

Makes 8 servings

Pisces Mexicana

Each serving contains 153 calories, 62 mg cholesterol, 2 g fat, and 90 mg sodium

2 pounds firm white fish fillets,
    preferably sea bass or red
    snapper
Juice of 3 limes
2 medium onions, peeled and
    thinly sliced (4 cups)
1 jar (4 oz) pimientos
3 large tomatoes, peeled and
    diced
1 tablespoon chopped fresh
    green chile
1 cup finely chopped parsley,
    plus 8 large sprigs parsley,
    for garnish

I developed this low-sodium Mexican fish recipe for the Canyon Ranch Spa the year it opened in Tucson, Arizona. It is good served with Portuguese Pilaf (see page 72), a salad with Fiesta Dressing (see page 44), and Poached Pears (see page 141) for dessert.

Wash fish in cold water and pat dry. Place fish in a glass baking dish and pour lime juice over top. Cover and refrigerate for at least 2 hours before cooking.

In a covered heavy skillet over low heat, cook onions until soft (about 10 minutes), adding a little water if necessary to prevent scorching. Chop half the pimientos. Add chopped pimientos, tomatoes, chile, and chopped parsley to onion. Cook, covered, until there is about 1 inch of juice in skillet (about 20 minutes).

Add fish and cook, turning once, until fish turns from translucent to opaque and is fork-tender (about 5 minutes on each side). Cut remaining pimientos into strips. Spoon tomato mixture over each serving and garnish with pimiento strips and parsley sprigs.

Makes 8 servings

Seviche

Each serving contains 81 calories, 31 mg cholesterol, 1 g fat, and 52 mg sodium

1 pound fresh white fish, cubed

½ cup freshly squeezed lime juice

Dash hot-pepper sauce

½ teaspoon freshly ground black pepper

2 cloves garlic, minced

1 large onion, peeled and minced (1½ cups)

¼ cup red wine vinegar

2 teaspoons dried oregano, crushed

½ cup finely chopped cilantro

2 medium ripe tomatoes, finely chopped (1½ cups)

1 can (4 oz) diced green chiles, with juice

1 jar (2 oz) chopped pimientos, drained

This classic dish is usually served with tortilla chips and presented as an appetizer. For a delectable variation spoon it over a bed of chopped lettuce and then serve it as a luncheon entrée with Toasted Tortilla Triangles (see page 122). Note that the fish must marinate in the lime juice for 24 hours.

Place fish in a large, nonaluminum dish. In a small bowl combine lime juice, hot-pepper sauce, pepper, and garlic. Pour mixture over fish, making sure that liquid completely covers fish. Seal dish with plastic wrap and refrigerate for 24 hours.

Add remaining ingredients; mix well. Refrigerate at least 3 more hours.

Makes 5 cups, about eight ⅔-cup servings

Paella

Each serving contains 367 calories, 113 mg cholesterol, 11 g fat, and 145 mg sodium

4 large shrimp (4 oz)

4 clams, in the shell (8 oz)

2 tablespoons extra virgin olive oil

2 cloves garlic, minced

2 whole chicken breasts (1 lb), halved, boned, skinned, and butterflied

1 medium onion, peeled and finely chopped (1½ cups)

½ cup uncooked long-grain brown rice

1 cup Unsalted Chicken Stock (see page 17)

¼ cup dry white wine

¼ teaspoon powdered saffron

⅛ teaspoon paprika

½ cup shelled peas (½ lb unshelled)

1 small tomato, preferably plum, diced (½ cup)

1 tablespoon freshly grated Parmesan cheese

1 jar (2 oz) pimientos, julienned, for garnish

4 lemon wedges, for garnish

Here is an ideal entrée for a buffet dinner party. It is truly a one-dish meal and looks so bright and beautiful it will bring raves from your guests before they even taste it. The chicken breast halves can be left in one piece or cut into chunks, as desired.

Peel shrimp, leaving tails attached. With a small, sharp knife, make a shallow slit down the back of each shrimp and lift out the vein. If it does not come out in one piece, use point of knife to scrape out remaining portions. Wash incisions well with cold water and set shrimp aside. Scrub clams with a stiff brush until they are very clean; set aside.

In a large, heavy skillet over medium heat, warm 1 tablespoon of the oil; add garlic. Add chicken and sauté until golden brown on both sides; set aside.

In a 14-inch paella pan, skillet, heavy casserole, or roasting pan at least 3 inches deep, heat remaining oil over medium heat. Add onion and rice and cook, stirring frequently, until onion is tender and rice is lightly browned (about 15 minutes).

Preheat oven to 400° F. In a small saucepan bring stock to a boil; add wine. Crush saffron and paprika together with a mortar and pestle and add to stock mixture; then add entire mixture to rice and onion, mixing thoroughly. Bring to a boil, then arrange browned chicken on top of rice mixture. Scatter peas and tomato evenly over top, then sprinkle with Parmesan cheese. Arrange prepared clams and shrimp on top. Set pan on floor of oven or on lowest rack and bake, uncovered, until all liquid has been absorbed by rice, rice is tender, and clams are open (25 to 45 minutes). Do not stir dish after it is in the oven.

Remove from oven, cover loosely with a towel, and allow to rest 5 minutes. Garnish with pimientos and lemon and serve.

Makes 4 servings

Stuffed Tarragon Trout

Each serving contains 313 calories, 62 mg cholesterol, 16 g fat, and 98 mg sodium

1 tablespoon unsalted corn oil margarine

2 tablespoons dried tarragon, crushed, or 6 tablespoons minced fresh tarragon

2 onions, peeled and very thinly sliced (4 cups)

2 rainbow trout (³/₄ lb each), split and cleaned

¹/₄ cup freshly squeezed lemon juice

Freshly ground black pepper, for sprinkling

Tarragon sprigs, for garnish (optional)

This recipe is a foolproof fish dish because you can leave the trout in the oven longer than the specified 20 minutes. Serve with Portuguese Pilaf (see page 72) and Savory Tomatoes au Gratin (see page 67).

Preheat oven to 500° F. In a large skillet over low heat, melt margarine. Add tarragon and mix well. Add onions, again mix well, and cook slowly until onions are soft (about 10 minutes).

Meanwhile, wash fish thoroughly in cold water, scraping any remaining scales off skin; pat dry. Rub fish inside and out with lemon juice. Sprinkle pepper over each fish, inside and out.

Place fish in a flat glass baking dish. Stuff each with ³/₄ cup onion mixture and spread remainder over top. Cover dish tightly with a lid or aluminum foil and place in center of oven. Cook exactly 3 minutes, timing carefully, then turn off oven. Do not open oven door for 20 minutes. Remove fish from oven and transfer to warmed individual plates or a serving platter. Garnish with tarragon sprigs (if desired).

Makes 4 servings

Poached Salmon
Each serving contains 155 calories, 40 mg cholesterol, 6 g fat, and 99 mg sodium

Unsalted Court Bouillon (see page 18)
Salmon (whole, half, or steaks)

For a spectacular meal, serve salmon with Sauce Hollandaise Sans Sel (see page 35), bright green vegetables arranged on the platter around the salmon, and Dill Bread (see page 126). For an equally impressive dessert, serve Cold Orange Soufflé (see page 146).

If you are preparing a whole salmon, use 3 quarts (12 cups) court bouillon and a fish poacher or a long roasting pan. If preparing salmon steaks or half a salmon, use $1^1/_2$ quarts (6 cups) court bouillon and a large stockpot. Pour bouillon into pan and bring to a boil over medium heat.

Wrap cheesecloth around fish, tying ends with twine and leaving cheesecloth ends long enough to lift fish out of bouillon when done. Place wrapped salmon in boiling bouillon. When bouillon returns to a boil, reduce heat and simmer fish until done, allowing 10 minutes per inch of thickness. Be careful not to overcook or fish will be dry and fall apart.

Grasping ends of cheesecloth, lift fish out of liquid carefully so it does not break apart. Unwrap and place on a warmed serving platter.

Divide into 3-ounce servings

Salmon Quenelles in Dill Sauce

Each serving contains 349 calories, 105 mg cholesterol, 25 g fat, and 89 mg sodium

1 cup Unsalted Chicken Stock (see page 17), plus stock for cooking quenelles (optional)

4 tablespoons unsalted corn oil margarine

1/8 teaspoon cayenne pepper

1 cup whole wheat pastry flour

2 eggs

2 egg whites

1 pound salmon, boned and puréed (2 cups)

1 1/2 cups Low-Sodium Dill Sauce (see page 38)

Dill or parsley sprigs, for garnish

Quenelles are simply poached dumplings, which are usually made with finely ground chicken, veal, beef, or fish. They have been a popular dish in Scotland for several hundred years. To make quenelles ahead of time, prepare them, let cool to room temperature, cover, and refrigerate. Reheat, covered, in a preheated 350° F oven for about 20 minutes. For more flavor cook quenelles in stock instead of water.

In a heavy saucepan over medium heat, combine the 1 cup stock and margarine. Bring to a boil, reduce heat to low, and simmer until margarine is melted. Remove from heat and add cayenne and flour all at once, stirring vigorously. Return mixture to low heat and beat until it forms a ball (which will take only a couple of minutes).

Remove dough from heat, transfer to a clean work surface, and make a well in the middle of the dough. Break 1 egg into the well, then mix dough and egg to re-form ball of dough. Repeat with second egg, then egg whites, then puréed salmon. Wrap resulting ball of dough tightly in aluminum foil or plastic wrap, and refrigerate until dough is chilled thoroughly.

With a sharp knife cut dough into 16 pieces of equal size. With wet hands form each piece into an egg-shaped quenelle. Place quenelles in boiling water or stock (if desired) to cover, reduce heat to low, and cook, uncovered, in simmering liquid until quenelles have increased in size and roll over easily when nudged with a spoon (about 20 minutes). Remove quenelles with a slotted spoon and drain well.

Place quenelles on warmed plates or a serving platter. Spoon dill sauce over top and garnish with dill sprigs.

Makes eight 2-quenelle servings

Fish Kabobs

Each serving contains 189 calories, 62 mg cholesterol, 5 g fat, and 94 mg sodium

12 boiling onions (³/₄ lb)
1½ pounds firm white fish, cut into 1-inch cubes
1 medium green bell pepper, seeded and cut into 1-inch squares (1 cup)
12 cherry tomatoes
1 cup Asian Sesame Seed Sauce (see page 39)

When time permits I like to marinate these kabobs for at least 24 hours before barbecuing or broiling them. Served on a bed of brown rice with a little of the marinade spooned over the top, they are delicious.

Peel onions and place in a large saucepan with water to cover. Bring to a boil over medium heat, cover, reduce heat to simmer, and boil for 5 minutes. Drain and allow to cool to room temperature.

On long skewers, alternate fish, onions, green pepper squares, and cherry tomatoes. Place skewers in a long glass baking dish and pour sauce over them. Cover and refrigerate for at least 4 hours before cooking.

Broil kabobs in the oven or cook over hot coals until fish is just cooked (3 to 4 minutes on each side).

Makes 6 servings

Fish en Papillote

Each serving contains 163 calories, 62 mg cholesterol, 5 grams fat, and 88 mg sodium

1 pound red snapper or any
  firm white fish
1 cup julienned carrot
1 cup julienned zucchini
4 tablespoons balsamic vinegar
8 sprigs fresh tarragon or other
  fresh herbs of choice
4 teaspoons unsalted corn oil
  margarine, plus more for
  sealing parchment
4 slices lemon

Cooking food in parchment or aluminum foil packets seals in the juices. It is a wonderful way to prepare fish over hot coals—just be sure you make the packets with aluminum foil, not parchment.

Preheat oven to 400° F. Wash fish in cold water and pat dry. Sprinkle with freshly squeezed lemon juice. Cut fish into 4 pieces of equal size. Use 4 sheets parchment or aluminum foil, each 12 inches by 16 inches; place on a flat work surface. Divide vegetables evenly among sheets of parchment, placing them in the center of each sheet; place a piece of fish on top of each serving of vegetables. Sprinkle each serving with 1 tablespoon vinegar, then on each serving place 2 sprigs tarragon, 1 teaspoon margarine, and 1 slice lemon.

If you are using parchment, spread margarine along outer edges. Fold parchment or foil over fish to form a packet, and seal by crimping edges with a tight fold. Place packets directly on oven rack and bake for 5 minutes. To serve, transfer each packet to an individual plate and carefully slit open to release steam.

Makes 4 servings

POULTRY

The white meat of chicken and turkey closely follows fish as a good source of animal protein that is low in fat and sodium. In this section you will find a variety of international recipes for poultry of all types. A recipes for rabbit is also included because rabbit more closely resembles poultry than red meat. It has all white meat, which tastes much like chicken and is lower in calories, cholesterol, and fat than any poultry. It is also low enough in sodium to be recommended for people on low-sodium diets.

When buying poultry always check the date on the package. Avoid torn or damaged packages and those that have an excessive amount of liquid. For the best flavor cook poultry within two days of purchase.

The single most important thing to remember when preparing poultry is not to overcook it. When you are roasting a chicken to serve as an entrée, place it breast side down in a flat roasting pan and bake it at 350° F until the liquid runs clear when the meat is pierced with a knife (about one hour). When you are roasting a chicken that will be cooled before use, remove it from the oven while the liquid is still running a bit pink. The chicken will continue to cook as it cools and you will have moist, tasty chicken meat to use in other recipes. Always remember to remove the skin and all visible fat before serving poultry.

Cornish Hens Orangeries

Each serving contains 240 calories, 81 mg cholesterol, 7 g fat, and 71 mg sodium

2 Cornish hens (2³/₄ lb total), halved
Corn oil, for rubbing hens
Ground white pepper, for sprinkling
1 large onion, peeled and quartered
1 cup freshly squeezed orange juice
¹/₂ cup dry white wine
1 tablespoon finely slivered orange zest
4 orange slices, for garnish

You can cook the Cornish hens ahead of time and reheat them just before serving in a preheated 400° F oven until golden brown. I routinely prepare Cornish hens in this manner because they are prettier, crispier, and tastier than when they are cooked just before serving. I like to serve them with Wild Rice à l'Orange (see page 73) and Zucchini in Basil "Butter" (see page 64).

Preheat oven to 350° F. Lightly rub hen halves with oil and sprinkle all surfaces lightly with white pepper. Arrange onion quarters in a shallow baking dish or roasting pan and place each hen half, cut side down, on an onion quarter. Bake for 15 minutes.

In a small saucepan over medium heat, bring orange juice to a boil. Boil until volume is reduced to ¹/₂ cup (about 25 minutes). Remove from heat and add wine and zest; mix thoroughly and set aside.

Remove hens from oven and set aside until they are cool enough to handle (about 15 minutes). With a sharp knife or kitchen shears, cut skin away from meat and discard. Place hens back on onion quarters, cut sides down. Pour orange juice mixture over hens and continue to bake 45 more minutes, basting frequently.

Remove hens from oven and place hen halves and onion quarters on warmed individual plates or a serving platter. Spoon sauce from baking dish over each serving. Garnish each serving with an orange slice.

Makes 4 half-hen servings

Pisces Mexicana (see page 87) is a south-of-the-border taste sensation. Green chiles impart just the right amount of spice, and the chopped pimiento and tomato give the dish a festive air.

Blueberry Mousse (see page 140), shown here with **Vanilla Sauce** (see page 42), is garnished with fresh mint, pineapple, and blueberries.

Fish en Papillote (see page 94) is shown here with julienned zucchini, summer squash, and carrots. Be careful when cutting open the packets—the trapped steam is released quickly.

Notched orange slices and julienned summer squash and zucchini make this **Chicken Curaçao** (see page 98) a feast for the eye as well as the palate.

Oven-Roasted Chicken

Each serving contains 130 calories, 64 mg cholesterol, 4 g fat, and 43 mg sodium

1 large onion, peeled and
  quartered
1 roasting chicken
1 teaspoon corn oil
  Ground white pepper, for
  sprinkling
  Garlic powder, for sprinkling

If the roasted chicken will be chopped for a later use, such as a salad, remove the chicken from the oven after about 50 minutes, instead of the hour specified in the recipe, since it will continue to cook as it cools. Allow the chicken to cool until it can be easily handled, then remove the skin and cut the meat from the bones. Refrigerate the chicken before cutting it into pieces; it is easier to cut into equal-sized cubes when cold. One skinned 3-pound chicken yields about 3 cups chopped cooked chicken.

Preheat oven to 350° F. Place onion in cavity of chicken. Rub chicken with oil and sprinkle lightly all over with pepper and garlic powder.

Place chicken, breast side down, in a roasting pan. Roast until liquid runs clear when chicken meat is pierced with a knife (about 1 hour). Let stand a few minutes before carving.

Makes 1 chicken; divide into 3-ounce servings

Chicken Curaçao

Each serving contains 165 calories, 49 mg cholesterol, 4 g fat, and 60 mg sodium

1 tablespoon unsalted corn oil
  margarine
2 teaspoons onion powder
3 whole chicken breasts
  (1½ lb), boned, skinned,
  and halved
2 cups freshly squeezed orange
  juice
2 teaspoons freshly grated
  orange zest
¼ teaspoon freshly ground
  black pepper
1 tablespoon grated fresh
  ginger
2 cloves garlic, minced
¼ cup curaçao
1 tablespoon cornstarch
1 tablespoon cold water
2 medium oranges, peeled and
  sliced, for garnish

This Caribbean-inspired chicken dish is delicious served with Mystery Slaw (see page 50) and Pineapple Muffins (see page 128). As I indicate in the variation, I also like this dish made with Pernod instead of curaçao. I serve Chicken Pernod with Zucchini Bread (see page 133) rather than with Pineapple Muffins and garnish it with sprigs of fresh anise, which emphasizes the licorice-like flavor of Pernod.

Preheat oven to 350° F. In a large skillet over medium heat, melt margarine. Add onion powder and mix thoroughly. Sauté chicken breasts until both sides are golden brown, and transfer to a baking dish.

In a small bowl combine orange juice, zest, pepper, ginger, and garlic; pour over chicken. Cover dish with a lid or aluminum foil and bake for 20 minutes. Remove from oven and pour curaçao evenly over chicken. Cover and bake 20 more minutes.

Place chicken on a heated serving platter and cover to keep warm. Place liquid from baking dish in a small saucepan over medium heat. In a bowl combine cornstarch and the water, mix until smooth, and add to liquid in saucepan, stirring well. Bring mixture to a boil, reduce heat, and simmer until thickened, stirring constantly. Pour sauce over chicken and garnish with orange slices.

Makes 6 half-breast servings

Chicken Pernod
Substitute grated lime zest for orange zest, omit the ginger, and substitute Pernod for curaçao in the previous recipe.

Chicken Egg Foo Yung

Each serving contains 168 calories, 136 mg cholesterol, 6 g fat, and 135 mg sodium

1 cup finely chopped cooked
   chicken
1 cup bean sprouts, cooked and
   drained
½ cup minced green onion
   tops, plus ½ cup chopped
   green onion tops, for
   garnish
2 eggs, slightly beaten
5 egg whites, slightly beaten
1 teaspoon corn oil
Sherry-Ginger Sauce
   (see page 42)

In this recipe, the beef stock in the sauce enhances the flavor. However, chicken or turkey stock can certainly be substituted. For an Asian feast serve this dish with Cantonese Sweet-and-Sour Pork (see page 116), Chinese Snow Peas and Water Chestnuts (see page 65), and Broccoli Stars (see page 60) with Asian Sesame Seed Sauce (see page 39). Accompany the meal with your favorite rice dish and a pot of tea, and pass fortune cookies for dessert.

In a large bowl combine chicken, bean sprouts, minced green onion tops, eggs, and egg whites; mix well.

In a heavy skillet over medium heat, warm oil. Wipe bottom of skillet with a paper towel to spread oil evenly over entire inner surface. When skillet is hot pour in ¼ cup egg mixture for each patty. Lightly brown each patty on both sides, then continue cooking until egg is completely set (about 5 minutes). Spoon a little Sherry-Ginger Sauce over each patty and then garnish each with chopped green onion tops before serving.

Makes four 2-patty servings

Chicken Paprika

Each serving contains 292 calories, 97 mg cholesterol, 12 g fat, and 100 mg sodium

1 tablespoon unsalted corn oil
  margarine
3 medium onions, peeled and
  finely chopped (4¹/₂ cups)
3 cloves garlic, minced
1 tablespoon paprika
2 medium tomatoes, peeled
  and diced (1¹/₂ cups)
1 frying chicken (3 lb), cut
  into serving-sized pieces and
  skinned
¹/₂ cup dry sherry
¹/₂ cup light sour cream

The first time I tasted a truly mouth-watering version of this dish was in a cellar café in Budapest. That memorable taste is recaptured in this recipe. For a complete Hungarian meal, serve Chicken Paprika with noodles and Caraway Cabbage (see page 70).

In a large, heavy skillet over low heat, melt margarine. Add onions and garlic; cook about 20 minutes, stirring frequently. Add paprika and cook another 10 minutes, stirring constantly.

Add tomatoes, chicken, and sherry to onion mixture. Increase heat to medium and bring to a boil; then reduce heat to low, cover, and simmer until chicken is tender (about 45 minutes).

Just before serving, transfer chicken pieces to warm individual plates or a serving platter. Add sour cream to sauce in pan and mix well, cooking just enough to heat sour cream. Spoon sauce over chicken and serve.

Makes 6 servings

Chicken Concord

Each serving contains 235 calories, 72 mg cholesterol, 7 g fat, and 69 mg sodium

1 cup unsweetened Concord
grape juice
1 tablespoon cornstarch
1/2 teaspoon fennel seed, lightly
crushed
1 tablespoon corn oil
2 medium onions, peeled and
thinly sliced (4 cups)
3 whole chicken breasts (1 1/2
lb), boned, skinned, and
halved
6 small bunches grapes,
preferably Concord, for
garnish (optional)

If Concord grapes are available, they are the most attractive and appropriate garnish for this tasty chicken dish. Otherwise, use any grapes that are readily available.

In a small saucepan combine juice and cornstarch; mix until cornstarch is thoroughly dissolved. Add fennel seed and mix well. Slowly bring to a boil over low heat, then allow to simmer until slightly thickened, stirring constantly with a wire whisk. Remove from heat and set aside.

Preheat oven to 350° F. In a large skillet over medium heat, warm oil. Add onions and cook until soft. Add chicken and cook until it is fork-tender and lightly browned (6 to 8 minutes).

Arrange chicken and onions in a baking dish; pour grape sauce over them. Cover and bake for 20 minutes. Remove from oven, divide chicken among 6 warm plates, and garnish each serving with a small bunch of fresh grapes (if desired).

Makes 6 half-breast servings

Turkey Cannelloni

Each serving contains 228 calories, 27 mg cholesterol, 6 g fat, and 117 mg sodium

$^1/_4$ teaspoon ground nutmeg

$2^1/_2$ cups Unsalted White Sauce, warmed (see page 33)

2 teaspoons extra virgin olive oil

1 medium onion, peeled and minced ($1^1/_2$ cups)

$^1/_4$ cup minced parsley

2 tablespoons chopped carrot

2 cups finely chopped cooked turkey

$^1/_2$ teaspoon dried oregano, crushed

$^1/_2$ teaspoon dried basil, crushed

$^1/_2$ teaspoon ground white pepper

$^3/_4$ cup dry white wine

8 Low-Sodium Crêpes (see page 134), warmed

$^1/_4$ cup unsalted tomato sauce

$^1/_4$ cup nonfat milk

$^1/_4$ cup freshly grated Parmesan cheese

Make this dish during the holidays or whenever you have leftover cooked turkey on hand. I love cannelloni, and this is my favorite cannelloni recipe.

Add nutmeg to white sauce and set aside.

In a large skillet over low heat, warm oil. Add onion, parsley, and carrot; sauté until vegetables are tender (about 15 minutes). Add turkey, oregano, basil, pepper, and wine. Simmer until wine is reduced by half (about 5 minutes). Remove from heat and add $1^1/_2$ cups of white sauce to turkey mixture and stir well.

Preheat oven to 425° F. Divide turkey mixture equally among crêpes, spreading mixture evenly down the center of each. Roll crêpes around filling; then place crêpes, seam side down, in a flat baking dish.

In a small bowl combine remaining 1 cup white sauce with tomato sauce and milk; mix well and pour evenly over crêpes. Sprinkle cheese over top. Bake until tops are lightly browned (10 to 12 minutes).

Makes eight 1-cup servings

Oven-Roasted Turkey

Each serving contains 148 calories, 62 mg cholesterol, 5 g fat, and 57 mg sodium

3 onions, peeled and quartered
1 turkey
1 tablespoon corn oil
Ground white pepper, for
   sprinkling
Garlic powder, for sprinkling

To make gravy for a turkey dinner, pour the drippings into a bowl and place it in the freezer while the turkey stands before being carved. When the fat has solidified on top (about 20 minutes), scrape it off and discard it. Use the defatted drippings to make Unsalted Turkey Gravy (see page 17), or store the drippings in the refrigerator to use later in stock or soup.

Preheat oven to 325° F. Place onions in turkey cavity. Rub turkey with oil, then sprinkle lightly all over with pepper and garlic powder. Place turkey, breast side down, on a rack in a flat roasting pan. (If you do not have a rack, place turkey in bottom of pan.) Roast uncovered until juices run clear when thigh skin is pricked (about 20 minutes per pound for birds up to 6 pounds and about 15 minutes per pound for larger birds). If turkey starts to get too brown, cover it with a piece of aluminum foil.

Remove turkey from oven, cover loosely with an aluminum foil tent, and allow to stand before carving.

Makes 1 turkey; divide into 3-ounce servings

Smoked Turkey Breast

Each serving contains 199 calories, 77 mg cholesterol, 6 g fat, and 68 mg sodium

1 tablespoon corn oil
1 tablespoon smoke flavoring
1/2 teaspoon garlic powder
1/2 teaspoon ground ginger
1/8 teaspoon ground white pepper
1/2 turkey breast (2 3/4 lb), with bone, skinned

Smoked turkey can be served either hot or cold and makes delicious sandwiches and salads. This is a special treat, as most commercially smoked meats are very high in sodium and forbidden on many low-salt diets. Try it on toasted Lettuce Bread (see page 125).

Preheat oven to 325° F. In a small bowl combine oil, smoke flavoring, garlic powder, ginger, and pepper; mix well. Rub mixture onto turkey, then place turkey in a roasting pan. Bake until turkey meat springs back when touched (50 to 60 minutes). Be careful not to overcook.

Remove turkey from oven; cut meat off bone and divide among 8 individual plates or a serving platter. Pour any liquid in pan over turkey before serving.

Makes eight 4-ounce servings

Lithuanian Rabbit

Each serving contains 300 calories, 77 mg cholesterol, 13 g fat, and 43 mg sodium

1 young rabbit (2 1/4 lb), cut into serving-sized pieces
1 lemon, halved
2 tablespoons unsalted corn oil margarine
3 cloves garlic, minced
1/4 teaspoon freshly ground black pepper
3 large onions, peeled and quartered
1/2 pound mushrooms, sliced (2 cups)
2 cups Unsalted Light Brown Sauce (see page 34)

This dish can be prepared to the point that it goes into the oven, then covered and refrigerated until time to bake it. Let the dish come to room temperature before placing it in the oven. For a savory and satisfying meal, serve this rabbit dish with boiled new potatoes and Baked Parsley (see page 67).

Preheat oven to 350° F. Rub rabbit with lemon. In a large, heavy skillet over medium heat, melt margarine. Add garlic and pepper and cook for a few minutes. Add rabbit to skillet, and brown thoroughly.

In a medium saucepan steam onions over rapidly boiling water until fork-tender (about 10 minutes); set aside. Add mushrooms to rabbit in skillet and continue cooking until mushrooms are tender. Transfer rabbit and mushrooms to a shallow baking dish and add steamed onions. Pour sauce over entire dish and bake, uncovered, for 1 hour.

Makes 6 servings

MEATS

Red meat, which contains a greater amount of animal fat than either fish or poultry, is usually limited in low-calorie diets. Veal is in a category by itself because it is lower in fat, slightly lower in sodium, and higher in cholesterol than beef. Meats that should be avoided completely in a sodium-restricted diet, because of the salt added in their preparation, include ham, sausage, bacon, corned beef, frankfurters, and cold cuts of all types. To replace this whole range of high-sodium meats, I have included a recipe for Low-Sodium Sausage (see page 115). In addition, I have created recipes for sauces (see Sauces, Gravies, and Condiments, beginning on page 28) that add the flavors usually associated with restricted meats to those meats allowed on a low-sodium diet.

When a recipe directs you to brown the meat, a very dark brown is meant; this heavy browning greatly enhances the flavor. When marinating meats in low-sodium marinades, marinate them at least twice as long as you would when using marinades containing either salt or soy sauce. Among the ingredients to avoid in low-sodium diets are meat tenderizer, monosodium glutamate, seasoned salt, soy sauce, commercially prepared teriyaki and barbecue sauces, and some of the commercial pepper mixes, such as lemon and herb peppers. When using herbs and spices in the absence of salt, it is sometimes necessary to triple the amount called for in recipes containing salt, so do not be alarmed by what may appear to be overseasoning.

Osso Buco

Each serving contains 317 calories, 100 mg cholesterol, 11 g fat, and 71 mg sodium

4 slices veal shank (about 2 lb)
1 cup dry red wine
1 can (16 oz) unsalted stewed tomatoes
3 medium onions, peeled and coarsely chopped (4½ cups)
3 cloves garlic, minced
2 bay leaves
2 teaspoons dried basil, crushed
1 teaspoon dried oregano, crushed
½ teaspoon freshly ground black pepper
¼ cup finely chopped parsley, for garnish
2 teaspoons freshly grated lemon zest, for garnish

When I had this dish in Italy, I was given a marrow spoon to remove the marrow from the centers of the bones. Those of us who are trying to cut back on the amount of saturated fat in our diet will appreciate this version of the zesty Italian dish and skip the marrow.

Remove all visible fat from veal. Place veal and ¼ cup of the wine in a heavy dutch oven or stockpot. Cover and cook over medium heat for 10 minutes, then uncover and cook until all liquid evaporates and meat is very brown (about 10 minutes more).

To the veal add the remaining wine, tomatoes, onions, garlic, bay leaves, basil, oregano, and pepper. Cover, reduce heat to low, and simmer until meat is very tender (about 2 hours). Uncover, increase heat to medium, and continue cooking until sauce is reduced by about half (about 1 hour).

Remove veal to 4 individual plates and spoon sauce evenly over each serving. Sprinkle 1 tablespoon parsley and ½ teaspoon zest over each serving.

Makes four 3½-ounce servings

Veal Oscar

Each serving contains 318 calories, 124 mg cholesterol, 24 g fat, and 115 mg sodium

18 spears asparagus (1 lb)
1 tablespoon unsalted corn oil
  margarine
6 small veal cutlets (1¹/₂ lb)
 Ground white pepper, for
  sprinkling
4 ounces cooked crabmeat
  (¹/₂ cup)
³/₄ cup Sauce Béarnaise Sans
Sel (see page 36)

This low-sodium version of the classic dish will pass muster with its most avid fans. This dish uses less crab than the classic version, since crab is high in sodium. I serve this dish with thinly sliced Swedish Rye Bread (see page 123).

Break off tough end of each asparagus stalk by holding stalk in both hands and gently bending stem end until it breaks. In a large saucepan steam asparagus tips over rapidly boiling water until crisp-tender (5 minutes). Remove from heat and immediately place under cold running water. Drain thoroughly and set aside.

In a large skillet over medium heat, melt margarine. Lightly sprinkle each cutlet with pepper, then place cutlets in skillet and lightly brown both sides. Continue cooking until cutlets are fork-tender, then remove from skillet and place on a baking sheet. Place an equal amount of crab on top of each cutlet.

Place 3 steamed asparagus tips on top of each serving. Spoon 2 tablespoons béarnaise sauce over asparagus. Place under broiler until sauce is lightly browned.

Makes 6 servings

Steak Au Poivre

Each serving contains 334 calories, 102 mg cholesterol, 21 g fat, and 73 mg sodium

1 lean, top sirloin steak (3 lb), 1¹/₄ inches thick
2 tablespoons black peppercorns, or peppercorns to taste
4 teaspoons unsalted corn oil margarine
¹/₂ cup dry white wine
1 tablespoon brandy

Because this classic dish does not include salt, it seems an ideal recipe to include in a low-sodium cookbook. I always prepare a 3-pound steak no matter how many people I am serving, because any leftovers make scrumptious sandwiches the next day served on Low-Sodium French Bread (see page 120). Leftover Steak au Poivre is also wonderful in salads, casseroles, and soups. I sometimes cut it into very thin strips and serve it over pasta or rice. The amount of peppercorns given in the recipe makes a very hot steak, so use less if you prefer a mild flavor. Note that the steak embedded with peppercorn is allowed to stand for at least 2 hours before cooking.

Prepare steak 2 hours before cooking. Remove all visible fat, then wipe with a damp cloth and pat dry with a paper towel.

Crush peppercorns with a mortar and pestle or wrap them in a cloth and pound them with a hammer. Place steak on a clean work surface. Press crushed peppercorns firmly into both sides of steak, then slap steak all over with the flat side of a meat cleaver to press in peppercorns more securely. Cover steak and allow to stand at least 2 hours at room temperature.

In a large, heavy skillet over medium heat, melt 1 teaspoon of the margarine, then wipe skillet with a paper towel. Increase heat to high. When skillet is very hot, add steak and cook for 5 minutes on each side for rare steak. For more well-done meat, cook it a little longer. Remove steak to a heated platter

Pour wine and brandy into the hot skillet and boil for 2 minutes, stirring constantly and scraping all drippings in bottom of pan into liquid. Remove skillet from heat and add remaining margarine. Slice steak horizontally into very thin slices and divide among 8 warm plates. Stir sauce well, then spoon an equal amount over each serving.

Makes eight 4-ounce servings

Martini Pot Roast

Each serving contains 327 calories, 90 mg cholesterol, 9 g fat, and 135 mg sodium

½ cup flour

1 teaspoon ground white pepper

1 lean pot roast (3 lb), preferably round-bone or 7-bone cut

1 teaspoon corn oil

1½ cups dry vermouth

3 cups Unsalted Beef Stock (see page 16)

2 tablespoons dried juniper berries

½ teaspoon dried basil, crushed

½ teaspoon dried marjoram, crushed

½ teaspoon dried thyme, crushed

2 bay leaves

4 small potatoes (1¼ lb), peeled and halved

4 medium onions, peeled and halved

4 large carrots (1½ lb), scraped and halved lengthwise

The name of this dish comes from the meat's being cooked in vermouth and seasoned, like gin, with juniper berries. However, I suggest accompanying the pot roast with a dry red wine rather than martinis! Juniper berries are available in specialty markets and health-food stores. This is an ideal make-ahead meal because the roast can be cooked ahead of time and be reheated while the vegetables are cooked with it. Serve it with a green salad and a dessert of fresh fruit for an easy, healthful, and satisfying dinner for any occasion.

In a large, sturdy paper bag, combine flour and pepper; add pot roast and shake until meat is completely coated with flour. Pour oil into a large, heavy skillet and place over high heat until pan is very hot. Transfer floured roast to the skillet and brown over medium heat, turning frequently, until roast is a very dark, burned-looking brown (about 1½ hours).

Add ½ cup of the vermouth to roast in skillet and simmer until vermouth cooks away. Turn roast over, add another ½ cup vermouth, and again simmer until vermouth cooks away. Turn roast over a third time, add remaining vermouth, and simmer until vermouth cooks away.

In a medium bowl combine stock, juniper berries, basil, marjoram, thyme, and bay leaves; mix well, then pour over pot roast, cover, and simmer for about 1½ hours. Add potatoes, onions, and carrots; cook until vegetables are tender (about ½ hour).

Makes 8 servings

New England Boiled Dinner

Each serving contains 250 calories, 78 mg cholesterol, 7 g fat, and 75 mg sodium

1 lean, fresh beef brisket (3 lb)
6 cloves garlic, halved
3 medium onions, peeled and chopped (4½ cups)
3 bay leaves
1 teaspoon black peppercorns
3 tablespoons pickling spices
4 small carrots (½ lb), scraped and halved lengthwise
4 small potatoes (1¼ lb), peeled and quartered
2 small heads cabbage (2 lb), quartered

At the Canyon Ranch Spa in the Berkshires in Lenox, Massachusetts, I serve this classic regional dish with Mustard Sauce (see page 32) and Swedish Rye Bread (see page 123). Note that cooked beef must be refrigerated overnight.

Place beef in a large saucepan or stockpot and cover with cold water. Add garlic, onions, bay leaves, peppercorns, and pickling spices. Cover with a tight-fitting lid and bring to a boil over medium heat. Reduce heat to low and simmer for 3 to 4 hours with lid slightly ajar so steam can escape. Remove pan from heat, let contents cool to room temperature, and refrigerate beef overnight in cooking liquid.

Remove and discard fat that has solidified on top. Over medium heat bring beef and cooking liquid slowly to a boil. Add carrots and potatoes. Cook until vegetables are almost tender (about 30 minutes). Add cabbage and cook just until cabbage can be pierced easily with a fork (about 15 minutes more). Serve hot.

Makes 8 servings

Enchiladas Hamburguesas

Each serving contains 233 calories, 47 mg cholesterol, 12 g fat, and 77 mg sodium

---

³/₄ cup Unsalted Beef Stock (see page 16), plus stock as needed

1 medium onion, peeled and finely chopped (1¹/₂ cups), plus 1 large onion, peeled and chopped, for garnish (optional)

1¹/₂ tablespoons chili powder

1 teaspoon ground cumin

3 medium tomatoes, peeled and diced (2¹/₄ cups)

¹/₂ pound lean ground round, cooked and drained

1¹/₂ cups grated low-sodium Cheddar cheese

8 corn tortillas, warmed

To create your own fiesta, start with Spicy Gazpacho (see page 22), accompany these enchiladas with Portuguese Pilaf (see page 72), and serve colorful fresh fruit for dessert.

Preheat oven to 350° F. In a large skillet over low heat, warm ¹/₄ cup of the stock. Add the 1¹/₂ cups onion and cook until it is soft and translucent, stirring frequently and adding a little more stock if necessary to prevent scorching. Add chili powder and cumin and mix well. Add tomatoes, ground round, and remaining stock; mix well and cook 5 minutes. Add ³/₄ cup of the grated cheese and mix thoroughly.

Spoon an equal amount of the mixture evenly down the center of each tortilla. Roll tortillas and place, seam side down, in a 7- by 12-inch glass baking dish. Sprinkle remaining cheese evenly over top. Cover dish and bake for 30 minutes. Remove from oven and sprinkle chopped onion on top before serving (if desired).

Makes six cups, eight ³/₄-cup servings

Mexican Meatballs

Each serving contains 110 calories, 32 mg cholesterol, 3 g fat, and 67 mg sodium

---

1 pound extra lean ground round

¹/₂ medium onion, peeled and minced (³/₄ cup)

1 slice bread, crumbled

¹/₄ cup nonfat milk

2 egg whites, beaten

¹/₄ cup minced parsley

2 tablespoons minced cilantro

1 teaspoon dried oregano, crushed

2 cloves garlic, minced

¹/₂ teaspoon freshly ground black pepper

2 tablespoons chili powder

In a large bowl stir together all ingredients thoroughly. Form mixture into 32 walnut-sized balls.

Makes 32 meatballs, eight 4-meatball servings

Irish Stew

Each serving contains 297 calories, 79 mg cholesterol, 13 g fat, and 117 mg sodium

2 pounds lean lamb, all visible fat removed, cut into 1-inch cubes (4 cups)

$^1/_2$ cup flour

4 teaspoons unsalted corn oil margarine

1 medium onion, peeled and finely chopped (1$^1/_2$ cups)

$^1/_2$ pound sliced fresh mushrooms (2 cups)

$^1/_2$ cup finely chopped parsley

2 cloves garlic, minced

2 bay leaves

1 teaspoon dried thyme, crushed

1 teaspoon dried summer savory, crushed

1 teaspoon freshly ground black pepper

2 cups water

2 cups dry red wine

2 turnips (1 lb), diced

16 small boiling onions

2 cups shelled peas (2 lb unshelled)

Although this stew is traditionally served in Ireland on Halloween with colcannon—a combination of mashed potatoes, cooked cabbage, and seasonings—for the luck of the Irish I like to serve it on St. Patrick's Day with Blarney Bread (see page 119) and St. Patrick's Day Potato Salad (see page 55) and decorate my table in shades of green. Stew is a wonderful meal for large informal parties because it is easy to double or triple the recipe without adding more pots. Also, it can be made ahead of time and reheated for your party. Leftover Irish Stew is good served over baked potatoes.

Place lamb and flour in a sturdy paper bag and shake until meat is thoroughly coated. In a large, heavy pan or stockpot over medium heat, melt margarine. Add chopped onion and mushrooms and sauté until they are tender. Remove from pan and set aside, then add lamb to hot pan and brown.

When lamb is a rich, dark brown, return onion-mushroom mixture to pan and add parsley, garlic, bay leaves, thyme, summer savory, pepper, 1 cup of the water, and 1 cup of the wine. Reduce heat to low and simmer, covered, for 1 hour; then add remaining water and wine and simmer for 30 more minutes. Add turnips and boiling onions and continue simmering for 1 more hour. About 10 minutes before serving, add peas and cook until just tender.

Makes 8 servings

Indonesian Barbecued Lamb

Each serving contains 370 calories, 113 mg cholesterol, 19 g fat, and 84 mg sodium

¹/₂ cup unsalted peanut butter
¹/₄ cup freshly squeezed lemon juice
¹/₄ cup dry sherry
¹/₄ cup sugar
3 cloves garlic, minced
¹/₂ leg of lamb, butterflied, all visible fat removed (about 3 lb)

The Indonesian lamb I ordered at Trader Vic's in San Francisco came with a peanut butter sauce on the side. I simply adapted the idea and made the sauce a marinade as well. Lamb chops can be substituted for the leg of lamb. Although barbecued lamb is best cooked over charcoal, it can be broiled successfully in the oven as well. Note that the lamb must marinate at least 24 hours before cooking.

In a small bowl combine peanut butter, lemon juice, sherry, sugar, and garlic; mix well. Place lamb in a container just large enough to hold it. Pour marinade over lamb, making sure lamb is completely submerged; cover the container; and refrigerate lamb for at least 24 hours before cooking, turning meat every few hours so as much marinade as possible is absorbed.

Remove lamb from marinade, reserving marinade to serve as a sauce for lamb. Cook lamb over charcoal or under the broiler, allowing 12 to 15 minutes per side for medium-rare meat, or more, to taste. Serve sauce warm, reheating if necessary.

Makes six 4-ounce servings

Minted Lamb Chops

Each serving contains 408 calories, 130 mg cholesterol, 24 g fat, and 90 mg sodium

4 loin lamb chops, 1¹/₂ inches
  thick (5 oz each)
1 lemon, halved
Onion powder, for sprinkling
¹/₄ cup Unsalted Mayonnaise
  (see page 37)
1 slice low-sodium bread,
  crumbled
2 tablespoons sugar
1 cup finely chopped fresh mint

These marvelous lamb chops can be prepared ahead of time, except for the baking. Your guests will think that only a magician could turn out this elegant entrée in just about half an hour. The fresh mint gives a more subtle flavor to the lamb than does mint jelly.

Preheat oven to 500° F. Remove all visible fat from lamb chops and place chops in a shallow baking dish. Rub both sides of each chop with lemon, then sprinkle both sides with onion powder.

In a small bowl combine mayonnaise, bread, sugar, and mint; mix well. Cover each chop with mint mixture, pressing mixture in firmly. Bake chops for 4 minutes, then turn off oven and do not open door for 30 minutes. Remove from oven and serve.

Makes four 4-ounce servings

Minted Rack of Lamb

This recipe works equally well for a rack of lamb. When cooking a rack, place it rib side down and pack mint mixture on top. Cooking time is the same as for chops.

Indian Lamb Curry

Each serving contains 284 calories, 86 mg cholesterol, 12 g fat, and 114 mg sodium

3 tablespoons unsalted corn oil
  margarine
3 medium onions, peeled and
  minced (4¹/₂ cups)
5 tablespoons flour
2 tablespoons curry powder
¹/₂ teaspoon ground ginger
2 cups Unsalted Chicken Stock
  (see page 17), heated
2 cups nonfat milk, heated
1¹/₂ pounds cooked defatted
  lamb, cubed (6 cups)
1 tablespoon freshly squeezed
  lemon juice

Serve curry over plain cooked rice with a large selection of condiments, such as Major Jones Chutney (see page 40), raisins, chopped unsalted peanuts, minced parsley, green onions, and chopped hard-cooked egg whites. People who do not wish to add calories with these condiments can try grated fresh orange or lemon zest on the side—either is colorful, delicious, and almost calorie free.

In a large saucepan or stockpot over medium heat, melt margarine. Add onions and cook until soft and translucent (about 10 minutes). In a small bowl, combine flour, curry powder, and ginger and add to onions, stirring constantly until a thick paste is formed.

Reduce heat to low. Add hot stock and stir until mixture again becomes a thick paste. Slowly add hot milk, stirring constantly. Continue to cook over low heat until sauce has thickened slightly (about 45 minutes), stirring occasionally.

Add lamb and lemon juice. Heat thoroughly and serve.

Makes 7 cups, 8 servings

Low-Sodium Sausage

Each serving contains 139 calories, 51 mg cholesterol, 8 g fat, and 40 mg sodium

2 pounds lean pork, all visible
  fat removed, ground twice
1 tablespoon dried sage,
  crushed
1 teaspoon each garlic powder,
  onion powder, and ground
  mace
1 teaspoon freshly ground
  black pepper
¹/₄ teaspoon each ground allspice
  and ground cloves

Guests seem to like this sausage better than the greasy, high-sodium variety available in the supermarket. If you have missed sausages for breakfast on your low-sodium diet, try these. I like to make them ahead and freeze them in individual plastic bags. This recipe works just as well with ground turkey.

In a large bowl combine all ingredients. Mix thoroughly, then form into 12 patties, about ¹/₃ cup mixture per patty.

To cook, place patties in a warm heavy skillet over medium heat and cook until browned (about 5 minutes per side). Drain on paper towels.

Makes twelve 2-ounce patties

Cantonese Sweet-and-Sour Pork

Each serving contains 360 calories, 51 mg cholesterol, 9 g fat, and 50 mg sodium

1 can (20 oz) pineapple chunks in natural juice, undrained
2 tablespoons cornstarch
1/3 cup cider vinegar
1/4 cup sugar
2 teaspoons grated fresh ginger
Dash cayenne pepper
1 tablespoon freshly squeezed lemon juice
1 pound cooked defatted pork roast, cut into 1-inch cubes (4 cups)
1/4 pound fresh mushrooms sliced (1 cup)
1 large green bell pepper, seeded and thinly sliced (1 1/3 cups)
1 medium onion, peeled and thinly sliced (2 cups)
1 can (6 oz) water chestnuts, thinly sliced
4 cups cooked long-grain brown rice, for accompaniment

This unique recipe captures a range of Asian flavors without using soy sauce. I like to serve it with steamed snow peas whose ends have been notched for a fancy look.

Drain juice from pineapple into a large saucepan. Add cornstarch to juice and stir until cornstarch is thoroughly dissolved. Add vinegar, sugar, and ginger; cook over medium heat, stirring constantly, until sauce has thickened.

Remove from heat and add cayenne, lemon juice, pineapple chunks, and pork. Mix well and allow to stand for 1 hour. Add mushrooms, bell pepper, onion, and water chestnuts; cook over medium heat until vegetables are just crisp-tender (2 to 3 minutes). Spoon each serving over 1/2 cup cooked rice.

Makes 8 cups, eight 1-cup servings

Italian Liver

Each serving contains 210 calories, 227 mg cholesterol, 6 g fat, and 60 mg sodium

1 teaspoon dried oregano, crushed
¹/₄ teaspoon freshly ground black pepper
1 cup dry red wine
1 pound calves' liver, thinly sliced
1 tablespoon corn oil
4 medium onions, peeled and thinly sliced (8 cups)

If you think you do not like liver, it has probably always been overcooked. Try cooking it medium-rare and serving it over pasta. I'll bet you will love it!

In a large, flat baking dish, combine oregano, pepper, and wine; mix thoroughly. Add liver and marinate for at least 2 hours.

In a large, heavy skillet over medium heat, warm oil. Add onions and sauté until golden brown. Remove liver from marinade and place in pan with onions. Cook to desired doneness, allowing 1 to 3 minutes per side for medium-rare. Remember, cooking liver too long tends to toughen it. Remove liver and onions to individual plates or a serving platter and serve immediately.

Makes 6 servings

BREAD, PANCAKES, CEREALS, ETC.

When I first started working on *Secrets of Salt-Free Cooking* more than 10 years ago, many commonplace foods, such as graham crackers and English muffins, were not commercially available without added salt. For this reason I included recipes for these basic items in the original book. Fortunately, many low-sodium products have been introduced since then and can now be found in most large supermarkets. Unfortunately, many commercial low-sodium products taste bland in comparison to their high-sodium counterparts. They often leave much to be desired in terms of taste and satisfaction. I have found that recipes requiring salt, baking soda, baking powder, and other high-sodium ingredients cannot be altered for a low-sodium diet simply by eliminating the offending ingredient. In my recipes I have added ingredients not usually found in many bread and bread-product recipes, that I feel improve the flavor and eliminate the flat taste often associated with low-sodium baked goods.

Here is an additional note on ingredients: Always check the expiration date on yeast packages. It is important to successful bread making that the yeast not be too old; if it is, the bread will not rise properly. Soften the yeast in water that is between 105° and 115° F. Cooler water will not activate the yeast, and hotter water can kill it.

A freshly baked loaf of bread is much easier to slice when it is cool. If you wish to serve the bread warm, slice the cooled loaf, wrap it in foil, and reheat it in a 350° F oven for 10 to 15 minutes.

Croutons

Cut 4 slices of any bread in this section into ¼-inch cubes. Spread cubed bread on a baking sheet and place in a 300° F oven until cubes are golden brown (about 20 minutes), stirring occasionally so cubes brown evenly. Makes 3 to 4 cups croutons.

Bread Crumbs

Arrange 4 slices of any bread in this section on a baking sheet and place in a 300° F oven until bread is very hard (20 to 30 minutes). Break into pieces, place in a blender container, and grind into fine crumbs. If you prefer toasted bread crumbs, make croutons, then grind croutons in the blender. Makes about ½ cup bread crumbs.

Blarney Bread

Each serving contains 83 calories, negligible cholesterol, 3 g fat, and 31 mg sodium

2 cups unbleached all-purpose flour, plus flour for kneading
1 tablespoon low-sodium baking powder (see page 164)
½ teaspoon baking soda
4 teaspoons sugar
4 tablespoons unsalted corn oil margarine, chilled
⅔ cup nonfat milk, plus milk for glazing
1 teaspoon freshly squeezed lemon juice
2 egg whites, slightly beaten
½ cup raisins
2 teaspoons caraway seed
Nonstick vegetable coating, to spray pan

Next St. Patrick's Day please your Irish friends with this low-sodium imitation of Irish soda bread. The traditional version of this bread is far too high in sodium for the recipe to appear in a low-sodium cookbook.

Preheat oven to 325° F. In a large bowl combine flour, baking powder, baking soda, and sugar; mix well. Add margarine and, with a pastry blender, combine mixture until it is crumbly; set aside.

In a small bowl combine milk and lemon juice. Add egg whites and mix again, then add milk mixture to flour mixture and thoroughly combine. Mix in raisins and caraway. Transfer dough to a floured work surface and knead until smooth and elastic (2 to 3 minutes).

Spray an 8-inch-round pan with nonstick vegetable coating. Place dough in pan and press it down so it fills entire pan. With sharp scissors cut a deep *X* in top of dough so sides will not crack while bread is baking. Brush top lightly with milk and bake until bread is light golden brown (35 to 40 minutes). Remove bread from oven and let cool in pan 5 minutes, then turn bread out of pan, place on a baking rack, and let cool to room temperature.

Makes 1 loaf, twenty 1-slice servings

Low-Sodium French Bread

Each serving contains 110 calories, negligible cholesterol, 1 g fat, 6 mg sodium

¼ cup lukewarm water
1 package (1 tablespoon) active
  dry yeast
2 tablespoons sugar
½ cup nonfat milk
4 teaspoons unsalted corn oil
  margarine
1 cup cold water
4 cups unbleached all-purpose
  flour, plus flour for board
2 tablespoons cornmeal, for
  sprinkling
 Boiling water, for pan
1 egg white, slightly beaten
1 tablespoon cold water

French bread from a bakery contains salt and is therefore not suitable for a low-sodium diet. You can easily make your own: The dough in this recipe requires no kneading.

Pour the lukewarm water into a small bowl and add yeast and 1 tablespoon of the sugar; set aside until yeast is soft. In a medium saucepan over medium heat, bring milk to full boil. Remove from heat and add margarine. When margarine has melted, add the 1 cup cold water; mix well. Add yeast mixture and again mix well; set aside.

In a large mixing bowl, combine the remaining sugar and flour; mix thoroughly. Make a well in center of dry ingredients and pour yeast-margarine mixture into it. Mix thoroughly but do not knead. Cover dough with a damp towel and allow to rise in a warm place until doubled in bulk (about 1½ hours).

Punch down dough and place on a floured board. Divide dough into 2 equal parts, then form each part into a long oval. Roll one long edge of each oblong toward center. Repeat with second long edge so that rolled edges meet in center. Taper ends of each loaf slightly with your hands. Rolling dough in this manner gives loaves a round rather than flat shape.

Lightly sprinkle an ungreased baking sheet with cornmeal. Place 2 loaves, seam side down, on sheet. With sharp, pointed scissors, cut ¼-inch diagonal slits about 3 inches apart across top of each loaf. Cover baking sheet with a damp towel and set it in a warm place until loaves are not quite doubled in bulk.

Preheat oven to 400° F. Place pan holding 1 inch of the boiling water on lowest rack in oven. Place sheet with loaves on center rack and bake 15 minutes. Reduce temperature to 350° F and continue baking until bread sounds hollow when tapped (about 30 minutes more). Just before bread is done, combine egg white and the 1 tablespoon cold water and mix well. Brush top of each loaf with egg-white mixture and continue baking 4 to 5 minutes.

Makes 2 loaves, forty 1-slice servings

Low-Sodium White Bread

Each serving contains 105 calories, negligible cholesterol, 3 g fat, and 12 mg sodium

1 cup nonfat milk, heated to lukewarm

1 package (1 tablespoon) active dry yeast

2 tablespoons sugar

2 egg whites, slightly beaten

$^1/_4$ cup corn oil

3$^1/_4$ cups unbleached all-purpose flour, plus flour for kneading

Unsalted corn oil margarine for greasing bowl, plus margarine, softened, for glazing (optional)

Nonstick vegetable coating, to spray pan

This is about as good as unsalted bread can be. An added bonus of baking your own bread is the wonderful aroma that wafts through the house while the bread is baking. I especially like freshly baked bread toasted.

In a small bowl combine milk, yeast, and sugar; mix well. Set aside, out of a draft, until yeast is soft.

In a large bowl combine egg whites and oil; mix well. Add yeast mixture and again mix well. Add flour, a little at a time, incorporating each amount thoroughly before adding more. Knead last $^1/_2$ cup flour in with your hands. Dough will be soft and sticky. Cover with a damp towel and allow dough to rise in a warm place until doubled in bulk (about 1 hour).

Place dough onto a floured work surface, punch down, and knead until dough is smooth and elastic (about 10 minutes). Form into a ball. Lightly rub a large bowl with margarine, roll ball of dough in bowl to coat with margarine, cover bowl with a damp towel, and allow dough to rise in a warm place until doubled in bulk (about 30 minutes).

Knead dough again briefly and form into a loaf shape. Place in a 9- by 5- by 3-inch loaf pan that has been sprayed with nonstick vegetable coating. Cover with a damp towel and allow dough to rise in a warm place until nearly doubled in bulk (about 30 minutes).

Preheat oven to 375° F. Bake bread until it is golden brown and sounds hollow when tapped (about 40 minutes). To glaze the bread, rub top of loaf with a little margarine 3 or 4 minutes before bread is done. Remove from oven, place pan on its side for 5 minutes, then turn bread onto a baking rack and allow to cool to room temperature.

Makes 1 loaf, twenty 1-slice servings

Continued on page 122—

Toasted Tortilla Triangles

Each serving contains 50 calories, no cholesterol, 1 g fat, and 40 mg sodium

12 corn tortillas

The advantage to making your own tortilla chips is that they are salt free and taste much fresher than the packaged, salty chips available at the market. These tortilla chips are also nearly fat free and are lower in calories than commercial brands. For variety, sprinkle them before baking with ground cumin, chili powder, garlic powder, or onion powder. They are best when freshly toasted.

Preheat oven to 400° F. Cut each tortilla into 6 pie-shaped wedges. Arrange wedges evenly on 2 baking sheets and bake for 10 minutes. Remove from oven and turn each piece over, then return to oven until they are crisp and lightly browned (3 to 5 minutes more). Remove from oven and let cool to room temperature on baking sheets.

Makes 6 dozen triangles, twelve 6-chip servings

Swedish Rye Bread

Each serving contains 61 calories, no cholesterol, 1 g fat, and 1 mg sodium

1 1/2 cups lukewarm water
2 packages (2 tablespoons) active dry yeast
3 tablespoons molasses
3 tablespoons sugar
3 tablespoons freshly grated orange zest
1 tablespoon each fennel seed and caraway seed
2 1/2 cups rye flour, sifted
2 tablespoons unsalted corn oil margarine, plus margarine for preparing pans
2 1/2 cups unbleached all-purpose flour, plus flour for kneading and for preparing pans

I often bake this bread in 10 to 12 tiny loaf pans, and serve each guest one whole miniature loaf of bread. The small loaves also make wonderful host or hostess gifts and are ideal for brown-bag lunches.

In a large mixing bowl, combine the water and yeast; set aside, out of a draft, until yeast is soft. Add molasses, sugar, zest, and seeds. Slowly add rye flour and margarine; mix well. Add the 2 1/2 cups all-purpose flour, a little at a time, working it in before adding more and kneading the last of the flour into the dough on a lightly floured board. Continue kneading dough until it is well mixed, then return dough to bowl. Cover with a damp towel and allow to rise in a warm place until doubled in bulk (about 1 1/2 hours).

Punch down dough, transfer to a lightly floured work surface, and knead until smooth and elastic. Return dough to bowl, cover with a damp towel, and again allow to rise in a warm place until doubled in bulk (about 30 minutes). Punch down again, transfer to floured board, and knead briefly.

Divide dough into 2 equal parts. Form each half into a loaf and place each in a greased and floured 9- by 5- by 3-inch loaf pan. Cover pans with a damp cloth and allow dough to rise in a warm place until almost doubled in bulk (about 30 minutes).

Preheat oven to 375° F. Bake loaves until they are a rich brown color and sound hollow when tapped (about 30 minutes). Remove from oven, place pans on their sides for 5 minutes, then turn loaves onto a baking rack and let cool to room temperature.

Makes 2 loaves, forty 1-slice servings

Low-Sodium English Muffins

Each serving contains 128 calories, negligible cholesterol, 2 g fat, and 14 mg sodium

1 cup nonfat milk, scalded

2 tablespoons honey

1 tablespoon freshly squeezed lemon juice

3 tablespoons unsalted corn oil margarine, plus margarine for greasing bowl and griddle

1/4 cup lukewarm water

1 package (1 tablespoon) active dry yeast

2 egg whites

1/8 teaspoon cream of tartar

4 cups unbleached all-purpose flour, sifted, plus flour for kneading

1/2 cup yellow cornmeal, plus cornmeal for sprinkling

I use these English muffins in my recipe for Eggs Benedict (see page 78).

In a large mixing bowl, combine milk, honey, lemon juice, and margarine; let cool to lukewarm. In a small bowl add the lukewarm water and yeast and allow to stand, out of a draft, until yeast is soft.

Add yeast mixture to milk mixture. In a small bowl combine egg whites and cream of tartar, lightly beat together with a fork or wire whisk, and add to milk-yeast mixture, blending well. Slowly stir in flour, a little at a time. Knead dough in bowl until flour is thoroughly incorporated.

Transfer dough to a floured work surface and knead until dough is shiny and elastic. Wash bowl, dry thoroughly, and lightly rub with margarine. Return dough to bowl and cover with a damp towel. Place in a warm spot and let dough rise until doubled in bulk (about 1 1/2 hours).

Transfer dough to a floured work surface, punch down, and knead again. Then let dough rest for 2 minutes.

Sprinkle 2 ungreased baking sheets with 1/4 cup cornmeal each. With a flour-dusted rolling pin, roll dough into a large circle 1/4 inch thick. Cut dough into 3 1/2-inch rounds with a biscuit cutter or lid from a wide-mouth jar, placing rounds on baking sheets. Form remaining scraps of dough into a ball and repeat rolling and cutting to make 20 muffin rounds.

Sprinkle top of each muffin round with a little cornmeal, spreading it evenly with your fingertips. Cover muffin rounds lightly with a damp towel and allow to rise in a warm place until doubled in height.

Lightly grease a griddle with margarine and place griddle over medium heat. Place as many muffin rounds as will fit on the griddle and cook until muffins are golden brown (8 to 10 minutes on each side). Transfer muffins to a baking rack and let cool. Repeat with remaining rounds.

Makes 20 muffins, twenty 1-muffin servings

Lettuce Bread

Each serving contains 119 calories, no cholesterol, 7 g fat, and 16 mg sodium

2 egg whites, slightly beaten
1/2 cup corn oil
2/3 cup sugar
2 teaspoons freshly grated
  lemon zest
2 teaspoons freshly squeezed
  lemon juice
1 1/2 cups unbleached all-
  purpose flour
4 teaspoons low-sodium baking
  powder (see page 164)
1/4 teaspoon each baking soda
  and ground mace
1/8 teaspoon ground ginger
1 cup finely chopped lettuce
1/4 cup toasted walnuts, chopped
Nonstick vegetable coating, to
  spray pan

For a dramatic-looking version of this bread, try making it with radicchio, the Italian purple-leafed lettuce, or substitute red cabbage for the lettuce.

Preheat oven to 350° F. In a small bowl combine egg whites, oil, sugar, zest, and lemon juice; mix well and set aside. In a large bowl combine flour, baking powder, baking soda, mace, and ginger; mix well, then add egg-white mixture and again mix well. Add lettuce and toasted walnuts and combine thoroughly.

Pour batter into a prepared 9- by 5- by 3-inch loaf pan and smooth top of batter. Bake loaf until a knife inserted in center comes out clean (about 1 hour). Remove from oven and let pan cool on its side for 5 minutes, then turn loaf out of pan, place on a baking rack, and let cool to room temperature.

Makes 1 loaf, twenty 1-slice servings

Dill Bread

Each serving contains 67 calories, 1 mg cholesterol, 1 g fat, and 97 mg sodium

1 package (1 tablespoon) active
   dry yeast
1 tablespoon sugar
1/4 cup lukewarm water
1 pint (2 cups) low-fat cottage
   cheese, rinsed (see page 75)
1/4 cup minced onion
2 egg whites, slightly beaten
2 tablespoons dill seed
1/8 teaspoon cayenne pepper
2 cups unbleached all-purpose
   flour
 Nonstick vegetable coating, to
   spray pan

This delightful savory bread complements any kind of fish or shellfish. I particularly like it served warm with cold soups and seafood salads.

In a small bowl add yeast and sugar to the water and allow to stand, out of a draft, until yeast is soft. Meanwhile, in a large bowl combine cottage cheese, onion, egg whites, dill seed, and cayenne. Add yeast mixture, then flour and blend thoroughly. Cover with a damp towel and allow to stand in a warm place until doubled in bulk (about 1 1/2 hours).

Preheat oven to 375° F. Stir dough until it is reduced to original size, then place in a prepared 9- by 5- by 3-inch loaf pan. Cover pan with a damp towel and allow dough to rise in a warm place until doubled in bulk. Bake until bread is golden brown (45 to 50 minutes). Remove from oven and let pan cool on its side for 5 minutes, then turn loaf out of pan, place on a baking rack, and let cool to room temperature.

Makes 1 loaf, twenty 1-slice servings

Gingerbread Muffins

Each serving contains 99 calories, 34 mg cholesterol, 1 g fat, and 13 mg sodium

2 teaspoons powdered instant coffee
1/4 cup hot water, plus 1/4 cup cold water
1/4 cup corn oil
1/4 teaspoon cider vinegar
3 egg whites
1 1/2 cups whole wheat pastry flour
1/4 cup sugar
4 teaspoons low-sodium baking powder (see page 164)
1 teaspoon each ground ginger and ground cinnamon
1/2 teaspoon ground cloves
1/2 cup raisins
1/8 teaspoon cream of tartar
Nonstick vegetable coating, to spray pan

One of my favorite breakfasts is a warm gingerbread muffin with low-fat ricotta cheese spread on top. Ricotta cheese is lower in sodium than cottage cheese and is a delicious, low-calorie substitute for butter or margarine on breakfast breads. Note that the egg whites are not beaten beforehand, because they are added separately.

Preheat oven to 400° F. In a small bowl combine instant coffee and the hot water and mix until coffee is thoroughly dissolved. Add the cold water, oil, vinegar, and 1 egg white. Mix well and set aside.

In a large bowl combine flour, sugar, baking powder, ginger, cinnamon, and cloves; mix well. Add coffee mixture and stir until well mixed. Add raisins and set batter aside.

Place remaining egg whites in a small bowl; add cream of tartar and beat until egg whites are stiff but not dry. Fold into batter, being careful not to overmix.

Spray muffin pans with nonstick vegetable coating—a total of twelve 2 1/2-inch-diameter muffin cups. Add batter to cups until each is about two thirds full. Immediately place pan in center of oven and bake until muffins are golden brown (about 25 minutes). Remove from oven and let muffins cool slightly before removing from pans.

Makes 1 dozen muffins, twelve 1-muffin servings

Overnight Oatmeal

Each serving contains 148 calories, no cholesterol, 5 g fat, and 3 mg sodium

2 cups rolled oats
1/2 cup chopped almonds
1 cup chopped raisins
1 teaspoon ground cinnamon
3 cups water

In addition to being the easiest oatmeal recipe I've ever prepared, this cold oatmeal is also the tastiest. It is even better if you wait two or three days before serving it. Try it with milk or yogurt or with cottage cheese and sliced fruit.

In a large bowl combine oats, almonds, raisins, and cinnamon; mix well. Add the water, mix well again, cover, and refrigerate overnight.

Makes 5 cups, ten 1/2-cup servings

Pineapple Muffins

Each serving contains 106 calories, no cholesterol, 3 g fat, and 6 mg sodium

2 cups unbleached all-purpose flour
2 tablespoons low-sodium baking powder (see page 164)
3 tablespoons sugar
2 egg whites
1 1/2 teaspoons vanilla extract
1/4 cup corn oil
1 can (20 oz) crushed pineapple in natural juice, undrained
Nonstick vegetable coating, to spray pan

These delectable muffins can be made, then frozen for future use. After removing them from the oven, let them cool to room temperature, then place them in airtight plastic bags in the freezer. The muffins are excellent for breakfast or with a variety of hot or cold dinner entrées. They are especially good with curried dishes.

Preheat oven to 425° F. In a large bowl combine flour, baking powder, and sugar; mix thoroughly.

In another large bowl combine egg whites, vanilla, and oil; beat lightly with a fork or wire whisk. Add crushed pineapple with its juice; mix thoroughly.

Add pineapple mixture to flour mixture; stir until well combined, being careful not to overmix batter. With nonstick vegetable coating spray muffin pans containing a total of eighteen 2 1/2-inch-diameter muffin cups. Add batter to cups until each is two thirds full. Bake until muffins are golden brown (about 25 minutes). Muffins may seem undercooked, but pineapple firms up as muffins stand. Let muffins cool slightly before removing them from pans.

Makes 18 muffins, eighteen 1-muffin servings

Whole Wheat Crackers

Each serving contains 30 calories, no cholesterol, 2 g fat, and negligible sodium

2 cups whole wheat flour, plus
     flour for kneading and
     dusting
¼ teaspoon each garlic powder
     and onion powder
Dash cayenne pepper
5 tablespoons corn oil
½ cup water
2 tablespoons sesame seed

These crackers are much more palatable than white soda crackers, and they are higher in fiber. You can substitute any seed you like for the sesame seed.

Preheat oven to 425° F. In a large bowl combine flour, garlic powder, onion powder, and cayenne. In a small bowl combine oil and water; mix well. Add oil mixture to flour mixture and combine thoroughly.

Transfer dough to a floured board and knead dough until it is no longer sticky. With a rolling pin lightly dusted with flour, roll dough out in a large square about ⅛ inch thick. Sprinkle seed evenly over dough, then press seed lightly into surface of dough with rolling pin.

Cut dough into fifty 2-inch squares. Place squares, well spaced, on nonstick baking sheets and bake until they are golden brown (8 to 10 minutes). Remove from oven and let cool to room temperature on baking sheets. Store in an airtight container.

Makes 50 crackers, fifty 1-cracker servings

Low-Sodium Graham Crackers

Each serving contains 37 calories, no cholesterol, 1 g fat, and negligible sodium

3/4 cup graham flour
1/2 cup unbleached all-purpose
  flour, plus flour for kneading
  and dusting
2 tablespoons honey
2 1/2 tablespoons corn oil
2 tablespoons water
1 teaspoon vanilla extract

The first time I made graham crackers and served them for tea, one of my guests said, "I didn't know you could make graham crackers—I thought they all came in a box." Not only can you make them yourself, but yours will be better than any store-bought grahams.

Preheat oven to 425° F. In a large bowl combine flours. In a small bowl combine honey, oil, the water, and vanilla; mix well. Add honey mixture to flour mixture and combine thoroughly.

Transfer dough to a floured board and knead until it is no longer sticky. With a rolling pin lightly dusted with flour, roll dough out in a large square about 1/8 inch thick. Cut into twenty-six 2-inch squares. Place squares, well spaced, on nonstick baking sheets and bake until they are golden brown (8 to 10 minutes). Remove from oven and let cool to room temperature on baking sheets. Store in an airtight container.

Makes 26 crackers, twenty-six 1-cracker servings

Giant Popovers

Each serving contains 131 calories, 1 mg cholesterol, 4 g fat, and 56 mg sodium

4 egg whites, at room
  temperature
1 cup nonfat milk, at room
  temperature
1 cup unbleached all-purpose
  flour
2 tablespoons unsalted corn oil
  margarine, melted
 Nonstick vegetable coating, to
  spray custard cups

When baking these popovers, be sure to spray the custard cups with nonstick vegetable coating to prevent the popovers from sticking; margarine won't do the job. You can delight your guests with enormous hot popovers without anyone realizing that you made them days ahead of time. After baking the popovers, let them cool to room temperature, wrap them tightly but carefully in aluminum foil or plastic wrap, and freeze them. To serve, remove the popovers from the freezer, unwrap them, and place them on a baking sheet in a preheated 350° F oven for 12 to 15 minutes.

Preheat oven to 450° F. In a blender container place egg whites, milk, flour, and margarine and blend at medium speed for 15 seconds. Do not overblend. Pour batter into six 3½-inch-diameter custard cups that have been well sprayed with nonstick vegetable coating.

Bake for 20 minutes. Reduce heat to 350° F and bake until popovers are golden brown and firm to the touch (about 20 minutes more).

Makes 6 popovers, six 1-popover servings

Giant Cinnamon Popovers
Add ¼ teaspoon sugar and ½ teaspoon ground cinnamon to blender container with other ingredients and proceed as directed.

Oat Bran Waffles

Each serving contains 123 calories, 1 mg cholesterol, 4 g fat, and 132 mg sodium

2 egg whites
1 tablespoon corn oil
1 tablespoon sugar
1/4 teaspoon salt
1 cup nonfat milk
1 1/3 cups oat bran
1 teaspoon low-sodium baking
  powder (see page 164)
Nonstick vegetable coating, to
  spray waffle iron

These waffles contain oat bran, the grain that has been shown to reduce serum cholesterol. Served cold, they are a fun and unusual alternative to bread for sandwiches.

In a small bowl beat egg whites until they form soft peaks, then set aside. In another small bowl combine oil, sugar, and salt; mix well. Add milk and again mix well.

In a large bowl combine oat bran and baking powder; mix well. Add milk mixture and stir until thoroughly moistened; do not overmix. Fold in beaten egg whites.

Spray heated waffle iron with nonstick vegetable coating. Use 1/2 cup batter for each waffle and cook waffles until they are deep golden brown.

Makes six 6-inch waffles, six 1-waffle servings

Zucchini Bread

Each serving contains 73 calories, no cholesterol, 1 g fat, and 16 mg sodium

1/4 cup chopped walnuts
1 1/2 cups shredded zucchini
1 tablespoon freshly squeezed
  lemon juice
1/2 cup sugar
1/4 cup corn oil
1/4 cup water
2 egg whites, at room
  temperature
1 teaspoon vanilla extract
1 3/4 cups unbleached all-purpose
  flour
3/4 teaspoon low-sodium baking
  powder (see page 164)
1/4 teaspoon baking soda
1 1/2 teaspoons ground cinnamon
1/4 teaspoon ground ginger
Nonstick vegetable coating, to
  spray pan

This bread tastes even better the day after baking. When the bread is cool, wrap it tightly in aluminum foil or place it in a plastic bag and store it in the refrigerator. To serve, slice thinly, wrap in foil, and reheat in a 350° F oven until bread is warm (8 to 10 minutes).

Preheat oven to 350° F. Toast walnuts on a baking sheet until they are golden brown (8 to 10 minutes). Watch carefully; they burn easily. Set aside. Decrease oven heat to 325° F.

In a small bowl combine zucchini and lemon juice and set aside. In another small bowl combine sugar, oil, the water, egg whites, and vanilla; mix well.

In a large bowl stir together flour, baking powder, baking soda, cinnamon, and ginger. Add oil mixture to flour mixture, then add zucchini mixture and toasted walnuts; blend well. Transfer batter to a 9- by 5-inch loaf pan that has been sprayed with nonstick vegetable coating. Bake in center of oven until a knife inserted in center of loaf comes out clean (about 1 1/4 hours). Remove from oven and let pan cool on its side for 5 minutes, then turn loaf out of pan, place on a baking rack, and let cool to room temperature.

Makes 1 loaf, twenty 1-slice servings

Low-Sodium Crêpes

Each serving contains 41 calories, negligible cholesterol and fat, and 23 mg sodium

1 cup nonfat milk
3/4 cup unbleached all-purpose
    flour
3 egg whites, slightly beaten
1 teaspoon unsalted corn oil
    margarine

I often make these crêpes ahead of time and keep them in the freezer to use with Crêpes Suzette (see page 149), Cottage Cheese Crêpes (see page 81), and Turkey Cannelloni (see page 102). To freeze crêpes, place a piece of aluminum foil or waxed paper between every two crêpes and wrap them well so that they are not exposed to the air. Before using the crêpes, bring them to room temperature and place them in a preheated 300° F oven until they are soft and pliable (about 20 minutes).

Place a covered casserole in a warm oven. In a medium bowl beat milk and flour with an egg beater or a wire whisk until well mixed. Beat in egg whites and mix well.

In a 6- or 7-inch cured omelet or crêpe pan over medium heat, melt margarine. When pan is hot, tilt it to coat entire inner surface with margarine, then pour margarine into milk mixture and mix well.

Pour in just enough batter to barely cover bottom of pan (about 2 tablespoons) and tilt pan from side to side to spread batter evenly. When edges of crêpe start to curl, carefully turn it with a spatula and brown other side. To keep crêpes pliable, stack in covered casserole in warm oven as they are cooked.

Makes 12 crêpes, twelve 1-crêpe servings

Low-Sodium Pancakes

Each serving contains 78 calories, 1 mg cholesterol, 1 g fat, and 67 mg sodium

4 egg whites
1 cup nonfat milk
*1 teaspoon freshly squeezed
   lemon juice*
*1 cup unbleached all-purpose
   flour*
*4 teaspoons low-sodium baking
   powder (see page 164)*
$^1/_4$ teaspoon baking soda
$^1/_8$ teaspoon ground mustard
*1 teaspoon unsalted corn oil
   margarine*

Pancakes served with light sour cream and fresh fruit are lower in calories than pancakes served with margarine and maple syrup—and they taste better.

In a small bowl lightly beat egg whites. In another small bowl combine milk and lemon juice; mix well. Add to egg whites and again mix well.

In a large bowl combine flour, baking powder, baking soda, and mustard. Add egg-white mixture and combine thoroughly.

Warm a heavy skillet or nonstick pan over medium heat until hot. Add margarine; when it is melted, wipe skillet with a paper towel. Use a soup ladle to pour 2 to 3 tablespoons batter into skillet. Cook until bubbles that form on surface of pancake burst. Flip pancake and brown other side. Repeat until all batter is used, removing pancakes to a warmed plate as they are cooked.

Makes sixteen 4-inch pancakes, eight 2-pancake servings

Gnocchi

Each serving contains 92 calories, 4 mg cholesterol, 3 g fat, and 53 mg sodium

2 medium potatoes (1 lb),
  peeled
1/2 teaspoon finely chopped
  garlic
2 egg whites, slightly beaten
1 cup unbleached all-purpose
  flour, plus flour for kneading
2 tablespoons plus 1/4 cup
  freshly grated Romano cheese
1 teaspoon extra virgin olive oil
2 tablespoons unsalted corn oil
  margarine, melted

This Italian potato dish is perfect with grilled fish, poultry, or meat. I also like to serve it as a brunch entrée with fresh vegetables and fruit.

Boil potatoes with garlic until tender; drain and mash. Place mashed potatoes in a large bowl. Make a well in the center of the potatoes, pour in egg whites, and mix thoroughly.

In a small bowl combine flour and the 2 tablespoons cheese; mix well. Gradually add flour mixture to potato mixture, a little at a time, until dough becomes stiff. Turn dough onto a lightly floured board and knead in remaining flour mixture, adding a little more flour if necessary, until dough is smooth but not sticky.

Divide dough into 2 parts. Roll each part into a long cylinder about 1 inch in diameter, then cut cylinders into 1-inch pieces. Press each piece of dough with your thumb to form a hollow on one side.

Preheat oven to 350° F. Fill a large pot with water, add oil, and bring water to a rapid boil. Drop dough pieces, a few at a time, into water. Cook until they float to the top, then remove with a slotted spoon, drain well, and place in 1 layer in a flat baking dish. Drizzle 1/4 teaspoon of the margarine over each and sprinkle the remaining cheese evenly over all. Bake for 15 minutes. If cheese is not lightly browned after baking, place dish under the broiler for 1 to 2 minutes before serving.

Makes 24 gnocchi, twelve 2-gnocchi servings

Low-Sodium Matzo Balls

Each serving contains 75 calories, 36 mg cholesterol, 4 g fat, and 34 mg sodium

1 egg, slightly beaten
2 egg whites, slightly beaten
1 tablespoon corn oil
¹/₄ teaspoon onion powder
¹/₈ teaspoon each ground white pepper and ground nutmeg
¹/₂ cup matzo meal
2 to 3 quarts Unsalted Chicken Stock (see page 17)

To serve the matzo balls in the chicken stock, divide the stock among six soup bowls and place two matzo balls in each bowl. This is the traditional method of preparation. To use the matzo balls for some other dish, such as Matzo Balls au Gratin (see page 83), remove them from the stock with a slotted spoon.

In a medium bowl combine egg, egg whites, oil, onion powder, pepper, and nutmeg; mix well. Slowly fold in matzo meal, being careful not to overmix. Cover and allow to stand for exactly 2 hours.

Moisten your fingers and form dough into 12 walnut-sized balls.

In a large saucepan over medium heat, bring stock to a boil. Place matzo balls carefully into stock. Reduce heat to low, cover, and simmer for 30 minutes.

Makes 12 matzo balls, six 2-matzo ball servings

DESSERTS

Interestingly, desserts, which create the greatest problem in most modified diets, present the least problem in a low-sodium diet. Fruits have a lower sodium content than any other food group as a whole, and fresh fruit is certainly one of the healthiest and most delicious desserts available in any diet program. This section contains many spectacular fruit-based desserts, a low-sugar fruit jelly (see page 157), and some unusual low-sodium sauces for fresh fruits.

Because I receive so many requests for dessert recipes, I have added a lot of variety to this section, including traditional American favorites such as pumpkin pie (see page 155), cheesecake (see page 156), and rice pudding (see page 147), as well as ethnic favorites such as Crêpes Suzette (see page 149) and zabaglione (see page 143). I have also included several of my own favorites, such as Cold Orange Soufflé (see page 146) and Peanut Butter–Honey Pie (see page 154). Both the Spiced Walnuts and the Fruity Granola (see pages 143-144) are welcome additions to brown-bag lunches and picnic baskets as well as delicious toppings for ice cream, yogurt, and salads.

Apple Dumplings with Brandy Sauce

Each serving contains 574 calories, 1 mg cholesterol, 24 g fat, and 57 mg sodium

2 cups unbleached all-purpose
  flour
1/2 cup unsalted corn oil
  margarine, cut into small
  pieces, plus 1 tablespoon
  unsalted corn oil margarine,
  softened
2/3 cup nonfat plain yogurt
6 medium tart apples, cored
  and peeled
1/3 cup sugar
1/3 cup chopped pecans
Nonfat milk, for brushing
  dumplings
Nonstick vegetable coating, to
  spray pan
Brandy Sauce (see page 42)

For a stunning finale to a dinner party, try these fancy fruit dumplings; they are lower in sodium, calories, fat, and cholesterol than the usual version partly because they use nonfat milk and yogurt instead of heavy cream.

Preheat oven to 400° F. Place flour in a medium bowl and cut in the 1/2 cup margarine until mixture forms coarse crumbs. With a fork stir in yogurt until mixture leaves sides of bowl and forms a ball.

Turn out dough onto a lightly floured work surface, and roll dough into a 12-by 19-inch rectangle; cut a 1-inch strip off long side of dough and reserve for decorations. Cut remaining piece of dough into six 6-inch squares. Place 1 apple in the center of each square.

In a small bowl stir together sugar, pecans, and softened margarine. Into the center of each apple, spoon 1 1/2 tablespoons of the mixture. Bring dough up around apple, brush edges of dough with milk, and seal seams well.

Spray a 15- by 10- by 1-inch jelly roll pan with nonstick vegetable coating. Place wrapped apples seam side down on pan. Brush with milk and prick dough in several places with a fork.

Cut leaf designs from reserved strip of dough. Brush underside of leaves with milk and place them decoratively on wrapped apples, pressing slightly so they adhere. Bake dumplings until apples are fork-tender and crust is golden brown (35 to 50 minutes). If crust browns too quickly, cover dumplings lightly with aluminum foil.

Remove pan from oven, transfer dumplings to individual serving dishes, and drizzle Brandy Sauce over top. Serve warm.

Makes 6 servings

Blueberry Mousse

Each serving contains 125 calories, 13 mg cholesterol, 4 g fat, and 19 mg sodium

2 envelopes (2 scant
  tablespoons) unflavored
  gelatin
1/4 cup cold water, plus 1/4 cup
  boiling water
3 cups fresh or unsweetened
  frozen blueberries
1 can (8 oz) crushed pineapple
  in natural juice, undrained
1 teaspoon vanilla extract
2 tablespoons sugar
1/2 cup light sour cream
Vanilla Sauce (see page 42)
Mint sprigs, for garnish
  (optional)

This ambrosial dish is my favorite mousse because it is so versatile. I like it for breakfast, with a fruit salad for lunch, and as a dessert after almost any type of meal. When serving it for dessert, I like to make it either in a large decorative mold or in individual molds and then top each serving with sauce and a sprig of mint. Garnish with additional blueberries and pineapple for an eye-catching treat.

Soften gelatin in the cold water and allow to stand for 5 minutes. Add the boiling water and stir until gelatin is completely dissolved.

In a blender container place 2 cups of the blueberries. Add gelatin mixture, pineapple and its juice, vanilla, sugar, and sour cream; blend until mixture is smooth. Pour into a large bowl, add remaining blueberries, and mix well.

Spoon mousse into 7 small soufflé dishes or one large dessert dish. Chill until firm.

Just before serving, prepare Vanilla Sauce. Spoon equal amount of sauce over each serving and garnish with mint (if desired).

Makes 3¹/₂ cups, seven ¹/₂-cup servings

Fast "Frozen" Yogurt

Each serving contains 82 calories, 2 mg cholesterol, negligible fat, and 61 mg sodium

1 envelope (1 scant tablespoon)
  unflavored gelatin
2 tablespoons cold water, plus
  ¼ cup boiling water
1½ cups plain nonfat yogurt
¼ cup dry instant nonfat
  powdered milk
¼ cup sugar
1½ teaspoons vanilla extract
3 cups crushed ice

This melt-in-the-mouth dessert is a great deal less expensive than store-bought frozen yogurt. It is also better for you. Because this yogurt has not actually been frozen and processed, all of its valuable bacteria are still active. Serve it soon after it jells, however; with longer storage the taste diminishes rapidly and the yogurt becomes watery.

In a medium bowl soften gelatin in the cold water and allow to stand for 5 minutes. Add the boiling water and stir until gelatin is completely dissolved. Let cool to room temperature, then add yogurt and mix well. Refrigerate just until mixture is firmly jelled.

Transfer jelled yogurt to a blender container and add remaining ingredients. Blend until smooth. Serve immediately.

Makes 3 cups, six ½-cup servings

Poached Pears

Each serving contains 162 calories, no cholesterol, 1 g fat, and negligible sodium

6 medium, firm ripe pears
  (2 lb), preferably Bartlett
4 cups water
1 tablespoon vanilla extract
½ cup sugar
1 teaspoon ground cinnamon
Ground nutmeg, for garnish
  (optional)

To serve the pears, place them on individual plates or in shallow bowls and either leave them plain, sprinkle them with nutmeg, or top them with vanilla yogurt or Low-Cholesterol Zabaglione (see page 143) or Amaretto Sauce (see page 142).

Peel pears carefully, leaving stems attached. With an apple corer remove core from base of each pear. In a large saucepan over low heat, combine the water, vanilla, sugar, and cinnamon; heat until liquid is simmering.

Place pears in simmering liquid and cook, turning frequently, until they can be easily pierced with a fork but are not soft (about 10 minutes). Remove pan from heat and let pears cool to room temperature in sauce, then cover pan and refrigerate all day or overnight. Serve chilled.

Makes 6 pears, six 1-pear servings

Amaretto Peaches

Each serving contains 76 calories, 1 mg cholesterol, negligible fat, and 38 mg sodium

6 small peaches, peeled and
   sliced (3 cups)
Amaretto Sauce (recipe follows)

When fresh peaches are not available, you can substitute either canned peaches packed in water or fresh-frozen peaches. Amaretto Sauce is also good on many other fresh and poached fruits, such as Poached Pears (see page 141).

Divide peaches among 6 sherbet glasses and spoon $1/2$ cup Amaretto Sauce over each serving.

Makes 6 servings

Amaretto Sauce

1 cup nonfat milk
1 tablespoon cornstarch
1 tablespoon sugar
$1^1/2$ teaspoons vanilla extract
3 tablespoons amaretto
2 egg whites, at room
   temperature (see page 164)

Pour milk into a small saucepan. Add cornstarch and sugar and stir until cornstarch is thoroughly dissolved. Place pan over medium-low heat and slowly bring mixture to a boil. Reduce heat to low, and simmer mixture, stirring constantly with a wire whisk, until it is slightly thickened. Remove pan from heat and allow mixture to cool to room temperature.

Add vanilla and amaretto to mixture and stir in thoroughly. In a small bowl beat egg whites until stiff but not dry; fold into sauce.

Makes 3 cups, six $1/2$-cup servings

Low-Cholesterol Zabaglione

Each serving contains 76 calories, 1 mg cholesterol, negligible fat, and 64 mg sodium

2 cups nonfat milk
2 tablespoons cornstarch
3 tablespoons sugar
1 tablespoon vanilla extract
$^1/_3$ cup Marsala
5 egg whites, at room
    temperature (see page 164)

This frothy sauce is as delicious as it is versatile. It can be served warm or chilled, presented in sherbet glasses or spooned over cakes, pies, and fresh fruits.

Pour milk into a large saucepan. Add cornstarch and sugar and stir until cornstarch is thoroughly dissolved. Place pan over medium-low heat and slowly bring mixture to a boil. Reduce heat to low, and simmer mixture, stirring constantly with a wire whisk, until it is slightly thickened. Remove pan from heat; add vanilla and Marsala and mix thoroughly.

Beat egg whites until stiff but not dry and fold into sauce. Serve warm or chilled.

Makes 4 cups, eight $^1/_2$-cup servings

Spiced Walnuts

Each serving contains 140 calories, no cholesterol, 9 g fat, and 7 mg sodium

$^1/_2$ cup sugar
$^1/_2$ cup cornstarch
4 teaspoons ground cinnamon
1 teaspoon ground allspice
$^1/_2$ teaspoon ground nutmeg
$^1/_4$ teaspoon ground ginger
2 egg whites
2 cups walnut halves

A cup of these nuts, wrapped decoratively, makes a welcome host or hostess gift. You can also make this recipe with other types of nuts, or mix spiced nuts with raisins for a healthy snack.

Preheat oven to 250° F. In a small bowl sift together sugar, cornstarch, cinnamon, allspice, nutmeg, and ginger. Mix well and set aside.

In a medium bowl lightly beat egg whites. Add walnuts and mix well. Dip each walnut in spice mixture to coat, and shake off excess. Arrange, well spaced, on a nonstick or well-oiled baking sheet and bake until they are lightly toasted (about 1$^1/_2$ hours). Remove walnuts from oven, let cool on pan, and store in a tightly covered container.

Makes 2 cups, sixteen 2-tablespoon servings

Fruity Granola

Each serving contains 121 calories, no cholesterol, 5 g fat, and 1 mg sodium

1/4 cup corn oil
1/2 cup sugar
1 teaspoon vanilla extract
3 1/2 cups rolled oats
1/2 cup almonds
1/4 cup each sunflower seeds,
   raisins, chopped pitted
   prunes, and chopped dried
   aprictos.

Granola is a delicious snack, breakfast dish, or topping for yogurt or ice milk. You can make it with other nuts, seeds, and dried fruits—experiment and create your own favorite granola.

Preheat oven to 325° F. In a large bowl combine oil, sugar, and vanilla; mix well. Add oats, almonds, and sunflower seeds and mix well.

Spread mixture evenly on a baking sheet with sides, or in a baking dish; bake for 15 minutes. Remove from oven and stir well, return to oven and continue baking until mixture is lightly browned (10 to 15 minutes), stirring occasionally to brown evenly.

Remove from oven and add raisins, prunes, and apricots. Let cool to room temperature, then store in a tightly covered container.

Makes 6 cups, twenty-four 1/4-cup servings

Kuchen

Each serving contains 163 calories, negligible cholesterol, 6 g fat, and 18 mg sodium

1 1/2 cups unbleached all-purpose
   flour
4 teaspoons low-sodium baking
   powder (see page 164)
4 tablespoons unsalted corn oil
   margarine, plus unsalted
   corn oil margarine, melted,
   to grease baking sheet
1/3 cup sugar
2 egg whites, slightly beaten
2/3 cup nonfat milk
1/2 teaspoon almond extract
1 1/2 teaspoons vanilla extract
Streusel Topping (recipe follows)

You'll win compliments if you offer guests this old-fashioned coffee cake warm with hot coffee or tea. You can serve it as dessert or as a sweet bread for breakfast or brunch.

Preheat oven to 350° F. In a small bowl sift together flour and baking powder; set aside.

In a large bowl combine margarine and sugar; cream together until fluffy. Add egg whites, milk, and extracts, mix thoroughly.

Add flour mixture to margarine mixture, a little at a time, mixing well. Stir batter until it is smooth.

In a 9-inch-diameter cake pan that has been greased with melted margarine, spread batter evenly. Sprinkle Streusel Topping over batter, and bake until cake is nicely browned (about 30 minutes). Let cake cool slightly in pan, then cut into 12 wedges and serve warm.

Makes 1 cake, twelve 1-piece servings

Streusel Topping

3 tablespoons sugar
1 tablespoon unsalted corn oil
    margarine
2 tablespoons flour
¹/₂ teaspoon ground cinnamon
¹/₄ cup finely ground or crushed
    almonds

In a small bowl mix together sugar, margarine, flour, and cinnamon until a crumbly mixture is formed. Add almonds and mix thoroughly.

Makes about ¹/₂ cup

Bananas North Pole

Each serving contains 105 calories, no cholesterol, 1 g fat, and 1 mg sodium

3 medium, ripe bananas (1 lb),
    peeled and sliced
1 teaspoon freshly grated orange
    zest, for garnish
Mint sprigs, for garnish
    (optional)

This easy, delicious, and dramatically beautiful dessert is both low in sodium and high in potassium. Rather than grated orange zest, you may wish to sprinkle each serving with ground cinnamon or nutmeg or anything else that sounds tempting and contains few calories and milligrams of sodium.

Place bananas in a plastic bag in the freezer until they are completely frozen and hard. Transfer them to a blender, a few slices at a time, and blend until they are smooth. Spoon frozen puréed banana into 4 sherbet glasses and garnish with zest and mint sprigs (if desired).

Makes 4 servings

Cold Orange Soufflé

Each serving contains 83 calories, 27 mg cholesterol, 1 g fat, and 36 mg sodium

2 envelopes (2 scant tablespoons) unflavored gelatin

1 cup cold water

2 egg yolks, at room temperature

2 cans (6 oz each) unsweetened frozen orange juice concentrate, thawed

1 teaspoon vanilla extract

8 egg whites, at room temperature (see page 164)

$^1/_2$ cup sugar

1 cup canned evaporated skimmed milk, chilled

1 tablespoon freshly grated orange zest, for garnish

I created the recipe for this exquisite dessert for Menu Magic, *a product book for SweetLite fructose. To substitute fructose for the ordinary table sugar (sucrose) used here, see the discussion of fructose on page 164. This soufflé can be made ahead.*

Fold a 24-inch-long sheet of waxed paper in half lengthwise; wrap around top of a 7-inch (1 quart) soufflé dish to form a collar that extends at least 4 inches above rim of dish. Secure collar with tape.

Soften gelatin in the cold water and allow to stand for 5 minutes. In a medium bowl beat egg yolks with a mixer or wire whisk until they are thick and foamy, then beat in softened gelatin.

Pour gelatin mixture into the top pan of a double boiler and place over simmering water. Cook, stirring constantly, until gelatin has completely dissolved. Do not allow mixture to boil. Remove pan from heat and stir in juice and vanilla. Pour mixture into a large bowl and refrigerate until it has thickened to a syrupy consistency (about 20 minutes).

In a large bowl beat egg whites until frothy. Slowly add sugar and continue beating until egg whites are stiff but not dry; set aside. In another large bowl beat milk until it has tripled in volume. With a rubber spatula fold whipped milk gently but thoroughly into juice mixture. Fold in egg-white mixture until no streaks of white show. Pour soufflé mixture into collared soufflé dish and refrigerate for at least 4 hours before removing collar and serving soufflé. Lightly sprinkle top with orange zest.

Makes 16 servings

Jamaican Rice Pudding with Rum Sauce

Each serving contains 204 calories, 54 mg cholesterol, 3 g fat, and 68 mg sodium

4 small bananas (1 lb), mashed
  (2 cups)
2 cups nonfat milk
2 eggs, slightly beaten
3 egg whites
¼ cup sugar
⅛ teaspoon ground ginger
1 tablespoon ground cinnamon
2 teaspoons vanilla extract
1 teaspoon rum extract
2 cups cooked long-grain white
  rice
Rum Sauce (recipe follows)

Each part of this recipe is scrumptious on its own. The rice pudding can be served warm with ice milk or Fast "Frozen" Yogurt (see page 141); and the Rum Sauce is good on any fresh fruit. I even like it on pancakes and waffles. Although the nutritional analysis for the pudding includes the sauce, a separate analysis appears for the sauce in case you use it elsewhere.

Preheat oven to 350° F. In a large bowl combine bananas, milk, eggs, egg whites, sugar, ginger, cinnamon, and extracts; mix well. Add rice and again mix well.

Pour mixture into a 2-quart casserole; set casserole in a deep pan that has been filled with boiling water to a depth of 1 inch. Bake until top of pudding is golden brown (about 1 hour and 20 minutes). Remove pudding from oven and serve warm with 1½ tablespoons Rum Sauce on each serving.

Makes 4 cups, eight ½-cup servings

Rum Sauce

Each serving contains 33 calories, no cholesterol, 2 g fat, and 1 mg sodium

1 tablespoon unsalted corn oil
  margarine
1 tablespoon flour
1 cup boiling water
2 tablespoons sugar
½ teaspoon ground cinnamon
1½ teaspoons vanilla extract
¾ teaspoon rum extract

In a small saucepan over medium heat, melt margarine. Add flour all at once and cook mixture, stirring constantly, for 3 full minutes. Reduce heat to low and remove pan from heat.

Add the boiling water all at once; stir with a wire whisk. Add sugar and cinnamon and return pan to heat. Simmer, stirring constantly with a wire whisk, until sauce is slightly thickened (about 5 minutes). Remove pan from heat and add extracts; mix well. Serve warm or cold.

Makes ¾ cup, eight 1½-tablespoon servings

Noodle Pudding

Each serving contains 211 calories, 52 mg cholesterol, 9 g fat, and 14 mg sodium

1/2 cup chopped walnuts

4 cups cooked flat noodles (8 oz dry)

1/3 cup sugar

3/4 teaspoon ground cinnamon

1 tablespoon vanilla extract

1/2 cup raisins

3 medium green apples (3/4 lb), unpeeled, cored, and very thinly sliced (2 cups)

2 eggs, slightly beaten

1/4 cup unsalted corn oil margarine, melted

Served warm and topped with nonfat plain yogurt, this is a favorite breakfast and a superb dessert. Your guests will be surprised and delighted to learn that pasta is so versatile.

Preheat oven to 350° F. Toast walnuts on a baking sheet until they are golden brown (8 to 10 minutes). Watch carefully; they burn easily.

Increase oven heat to 375° F. In a large bowl combine toasted walnuts, noodles, sugar, cinnamon, vanilla, raisins, apples, and eggs; mix thoroughly. Transfer mixture to a 2-quart casserole or baking dish and pour margarine evenly over top. Bake until top of pudding is golden brown (about 45 minutes).

Makes 8 cups, twelve 2/3-cup servings

Crêpes Suzette
Each serving contains 159 calories, 1 mg cholesterol, 3 g fat, and 49 mg sodium

1 cup freshly squeezed orange juice
2 teaspoons cornstarch
3 tablespoons sugar
1 tablespoon freshly grated orange zest
¼ cup orange-flavored liqueur
1 tablespoon unsalted corn oil margarine
12 Low-Sodium Crêpes (see page 134), warmed
2 tablespoons brandy (optional)

For a truly dramatic presentation, you can add brandy to the sauce remaining in the chafing dish and ignite it with a match. Shake the chafing dish gently back and forth while you carefully spoon the flaming liquid over the folded crêpes.

Pour orange juice into a small saucepan. Add cornstarch and 2 tablespoons of the sugar; stir until cornstarch is dissolved. Over medium-low heat slowly bring to a boil. Reduce heat to low and simmer mixture, stirring constantly with a wire whisk, until mixture is slightly thickened (about 5 minutes).

Remove pan from heat and add zest, liqueur, and margarine. Stir until margarine has completely melted, then pour sauce into a heated chafing dish.

Dip both sides of each crêpe in sauce; fold in half, then fold in half crosswise, forming a triangle. Push folded crêpes to side of chafing dish to soak up sauce, then arrange them on a warmed serving plate as they become crowded in the dish. Sprinkle remaining sugar evenly over crêpes when they have all been transferred to serving plate.

Makes 12 crêpes, six 2-crêpe servings

Low-Sodium Cream Puffs

Each unfilled cream puff contains 86 calories, no cholesterol, 6 g fat, and 15 mg sodium

$1/2$ cup water

4 tablespoons unsalted corn oil margarine

$1/2$ cup unbleached all-purpose flour

2 teaspoons sugar (see Note, below)

1 egg

2 egg whites

Nonstick vegetable coating, to spray baking sheet

Golden Filling or Savory Filling (see page 151)

8 thin orange slices, with rind (for garnish with Golden Filling) or 4 teaspoons drained sun-dried tomatoes (for garnish with Savory Filling), optional

These cream puffs with Golden Filling or Savory Filling (see page 151) are superb for dessert or on a breakfast or brunch menu. To make small cream puffs, simply make 16 mounds of batter on the baking sheet, instead of 8, and reduce the cooking time by about 10 minutes.

Preheat oven to 375° F. In a small saucepan over medium heat, combine the water and margarine and bring to a boil.

In a small bowl combine flour and sugar and add all at once to the boiling liquid. Reduce heat to low, mix well, and beat until mixture leaves sides of pan and forms a ball. Remove from heat and let cool slightly (about 5 minutes).

Add egg and mix well; add egg whites, one at a time, beating well after each addition. Continue beating until mixture has a satinlike sheen.

On a large baking sheet sprayed with nonstick vegetable coating, arrange 8 equal mounds of batter about 2 inches apart; make a decorative pattern on top of each mound. Bake until cream puffs are nicely browned and puffy (40 to 45 minutes). Remove pan from oven and immediately cut a slit in the side of each puff. Return pan to oven and bake cream puffs until they are golden brown (8 to 10 more minutes).

Remove pan from oven and let cream puffs cool on a wire rack.

Prepare filling of choice. To serve, either split puffs almost all the way around or slice top off each puff. Spoon filling evenly over bottom portion of each cream puff. Place top portion on each puff and garnish (if desired).

Makes 8 cream puffs, eight 1-puff servings

Note Omit sugar when filling cream puffs with Savory Filling.

Golden Filling

Each serving contains 147 calories, 19 mg cholesterol, 5 g fat, and 53 mg sodium

1 can (6 oz) unsweetened
  frozen orange juice
  concentrate, thawed
1 pound (2 cups) low-fat
  ricotta cheese, rinsed (see
  page 75)
$1/4$ cup sugar
$1^1/2$ teaspoons vanilla extract

In a large bowl combine juice, ricotta, sugar, and vanilla. With a wire whisk beat mixture until it is smooth and light in texture.

Makes about $2^2/3$ cups, eight $1/3$-cup servings

Savory Filling

Each serving contains 90 calories, 19 mg cholesterol, 5 g fat, and 60 mg sodium

6 ounces low-sodium vegetable
  juice
1 pound (2 cups) low-fat
  ricotta cheese, rinsed (see
  page 75)
$1^1/2$ teaspoons low-sodium
  Worcestershire sauce

Prepare Low-Sodium Cream Puffs (see page 150) without sugar.

In a large bowl combine juice, ricotta, and Worcestershire sauce. With a wire whisk beat mixture until it is smooth and light in texture.

Makes about $2^2/3$ cups, eight $1/3$-cup servings

Strawberries Hoffmann–La Roche

Each serving contains 80 calories, 1 mg cholesterol, negligible fat, and 44 mg sodium

1 cup nonfat milk
1 tablespoon cornstarch
2 tablespoons sugar
1 1/2 teaspoons vanilla extract
2 tablespoons orange-flavored liqueur
2 egg whites, at room temperature (see page 164)
1/8 teaspoon cream of tartar
2 pints fresh strawberries, sliced (4 cups), plus 6 whole strawberries, for garnish

I created this dessert for a dinner party given by Hoffmann–La Roche, Inc., at Joseph's Restaurant in Boston. In addition to being a lovely end to a meal, this dish is also very low in sodium.

Pour milk into a large saucepan. Add cornstarch and sugar and stir until cornstarch is thoroughly dissolved. Place pan over medium-low heat and slowly bring mixture to a boil. Reduce heat to low, and simmer mixture, stirring constantly with a wire whisk, until it is slightly thickened. Remove pan from heat and let mixture cool to room temperature.

Add vanilla and liqueur to cooled mixture and stir until well blended. In a small bowl combine egg whites and cream of tartar and beat egg whites until stiff but not dry. Fold egg whites into liqueur mixture, then add sliced strawberries and mix gently but thoroughly. Divide among 6 sherbet glasses; garnish each serving with a whole strawberry.

Makes 3 cups, six 1/2-cup servings

Dieter's Dream Fruitcake

Each serving contains 115 calories, negligible cholesterol, 5 g fat, and 11 mg sodium

1   envelope (1 scant tablespoon)
    unflavored gelatin
2   tablespoons cold water, plus
    $1/4$ cup boiling water
$1/2$ cup nonfat milk
$1/2$ cup unsweetened applesauce
$1/2$ cup raisins
$1/2$ teaspoon ground cinnamon
$1/4$ teaspoon ground allspice
$1/8$ teaspoon ground nutmeg
$1/2$ teaspoon carob powder or
    unsweetened cocoa powder
1   teaspoon vanilla extract
1   can (8 oz) crushed pineapple
    in natural juice, drained
$1/2$ cup chopped walnuts

With all the traditional flavors associated with the original holiday favorite and only a fraction of the calories, this fruitcake truly is a dieter's dream. Note that fruitcake must be chilled several hours or overnight.

In a small bowl soften gelatin in the cold water and allow to stand for 5 minutes. Add the boiling water and stir until gelatin is completely dissolved. Pour gelatin into a blender container and add milk, applesauce, raisins, cinnamon, allspice, nutmeg, carob powder, and vanilla. Blend until ingredients are thoroughly mixed and raisins are coarsely chopped.

Pour blended mixture into a large bowl and add pineapple; mix thoroughly. Pour into an oiled 9-inch-diameter cake pan and refrigerate until firm (several hours or overnight).

Just before serving fruitcake, preheat oven to 350° F. Toast walnuts on a baking sheet until they are golden brown (8 to 10 minutes). Watch carefully; they burn easily. Set aside.

Remove fruitcake from refrigerator. Place a cake plate over top of cake pan and quickly invert fruitcake onto plate. Sprinkle toasted walnuts evenly over cake.

Makes 1 cake, 8 servings

Perfect Salt-Free Pie Crust

Each serving contains 115 calories, no cholesterol, 7 g fat, and negligible sodium

1   cup whole wheat pastry flour
¹/₄ cup corn oil
3   tablespoons ice water
¹/₄ teaspoon cider vinegar

I developed this method for making pie crust while working on the Fabulous Fiber Cookbook. *The recipe continues to appear in my books because it is the easiest, least messy method I know for making a good pie crust. It really is "perfect." If your recipe calls for a prebaked crust, see* Note.

Place flour in a 9-inch pie pan. Measure oil in a large measuring cup, add the water and vinegar and mix well with a fork. Slowly add oil mixture to flour in pie pan, mixing with fork. Continue mixing until all ingredients are well blended.

With your fingers press dough to cover entire inner surface of pan evenly. Crust is now ready to be filled or baked.

Makes one 9-inch pie crust, 8 servings

Note For a baked crust, prick bottom of dough with a fork in several places and place in preheated 375° F oven until crust is golden brown (20 to 25 minutes).

Peanut Butter–Honey Pie

Each serving contains 253 calories, 1 mg cholesterol, 15 g fat, and 28 mg sodium

1   envelope (1 scant tablespoon) unflavored gelatin
2   tablespoons cold water, plus ¹/₄ cup boiling water
1¹/₂ cups nonfat milk
¹/₂ cup creamy unsalted peanut butter
3   tablespoons honey
1¹/₂ teaspoons vanilla extract
1   Perfect Salt-Free Pie Crust (see above), prebaked
Ground cinnamon, for garnish

Anyone familiar with my other cookbooks knows how much I love peanut butter—plain, in punch, cookies, salad dressings, or pie. This pie is my all-time favorite dessert.

In a small bowl soften gelatin in the cold water and allow to stand for 5 minutes. Add the boiling water and stir until gelatin is completely dissolved. Transfer gelatin to a blender container and add milk, peanut butter, honey, and vanilla. Blend until mixture is smooth and frothy.

Pour mixture into pie shell and sprinkle lightly with cinnamon. Refrigerate until filling is firm.

Makes one 9-inch pie, 8 servings

Perfect Pumpkin Pie

Each serving contains 203 calories, 1 mg cholesterol, 10 g fat, and 20 mg sodium

¹/₄ cup chopped walnuts
1 envelope (1 scant tablespoon) unflavored gelatin
2 tablespoons cold water, plus ¹/₄ cup boiling water
1 can (16 oz) mashed cooked pumpkin
1¹/₂ teaspoons ground cinnamon
¹/₂ teaspoon ground ginger
¹/₄ teaspoon ground cloves
¹/₄ cup sugar
2 teaspoons vanilla extract
1 cup nonfat milk
1 Perfect Salt-Free Pie Crust (see page 154), prebaked

I stole the title from my own pie crust recipe for this pumpkin pie because it is the fastest, easiest pumpkin pie I know. It is also one of the most delicious, and it is certainly lower in calories than any other pumpkin pie I have ever eaten.

Preheat oven to 350° F. Toast walnuts on a baking sheet until they are golden brown (8 to 10 minutes). Watch carefully; they burn easily. Set aside.

In a small bowl soften gelatin in the cold water and allow to stand for 5 minutes. Add the boiling water and stir until gelatin is completely dissolved. Transfer gelatin to a blender container and add pumpkin, cinnamon, ginger, cloves, sugar, vanilla, and milk; blend until mixture is frothy. Let filling stand until it is slightly thickened (about 15 minutes), then pour into baked pie shell.

Refrigerate pie until filling is firm. Sprinkle toasted walnuts evenly over top before serving.

Makes one 9-inch pie, 8 servings

Cinnamon-Lemon Cheesecake

Each serving contains 136 calories, 31 mg cholesterol, 6 g fat, and 90 mg sodium

1/2 cup graham cracker crumbs (8 Low-Sodium Graham Crackers, see page 130)

2 tablespoons unsalted corn oil margarine, at room temperature

1 pound (2 cups) low-fat ricotta cheese, rinsed (see page 75)

1/3 cup sugar

2 tablespoons flour

2 teaspoons ground cinnamon

1 egg yolk, at room temperature

1/2 cup canned evaporated skimmed milk

2 teaspoons vanilla extract

2 teaspoons freshly grated lemon zest

3 egg whites, at room temperature

1/8 teaspoon cream of tartar

The graham cracker crust makes such a beautiful topping that I often serve this "upside-down" cheesecake as a birthday cake decorated with fresh fruit and candles.

Preheat oven to 325° F. In a small bowl combine graham cracker crumbs and margarine; mix well. Press mixture evenly into bottom of a nonstick or well-greased 9-inch-diameter cake pan; set aside.

In a blender container combine ricotta, sugar, flour, cinnamon, egg yolk, milk, vanilla, and zest; blend to a smooth, creamy consistency. Pour mixture into a large mixing bowl and set aside.

In a medium bowl combine egg whites and cream of tartar and beat until egg whites are stiff but not dry. Fold into ricotta mixture, then pour batter into graham cracker crust. Bake in center of oven until cheesecake is lightly browned (45 to 50 minutes). Remove from oven and let cool in pan on a wire rack. Loosen sides of cheesecake from pan with the tip of a sharp knife. Then place a plate over top of pan and quickly invert cake onto plate. Cover with plastic wrap and chill before serving.

Makes 1 cheesecake, 12 servings

Strawberry Jelly
Each serving contains 17 calories, no cholesterol, and negligible fat and sodium

2 teaspoons unflavored gelatin
2 tablespoons cool water
4 cups strawberries, washed and
    stems removed
3 tablespoons sugar

This easy-to-make jelly contains much less sugar than commercial preparations and can be made with frozen unsweetened strawberries when fresh berries are not in season. It will keep two to three weeks in the refrigerator.

In a small bowl combine gelatin and the water; set aside.

Place strawberries in a large saucepan and mash thoroughly. Stir in sugar, cover pan, and cook over low heat for 5 minutes. Pour hot mixture into softened gelatin and stir until gelatin completely dissolves.

Transfer strawberry mixture to a blender container and blend until it is smooth. Refrigerate in a covered container.

Makes 2¹/₂ cups, twenty 2-tablespoon servings

BEVERAGES

Calorie counters will be happy with this beverage section. It has low-calorie Desert Tea (see page 162) for teetotalers and a Counterfeit Cocktail (see page 159) for cocktail-party goers who can't afford extra calories before dinner. For those who enjoy a glass or two of wine with dinner but don't want the added calories, or a morning-after headache, Calorie Counter's Wine (see page 160) tells you how to remove the alcohol from wine!

Many unusual, refreshing fruit drinks are also included, together with a Vitality Cocktail (see page 159) for people who prefer to drink their breakfast. Because my favorite beverage is peanut butter punch, I have included a low-sodium variation (see page 163).

Drinking plenty of water is one of the best things we can do for our health. Many people are afraid that drinking too much water will cause them to become bloated; yet the opposite is true. The more water we drink, the more efficiently we excrete it. It is just like priming a pump.

If the water in your area is high in sodium or has an objectionable taste or odor, you may unconsciously be drinking less than you need for optimum health. If this is the case, try drinking distilled water or any of the low-sodium bottled waters that are available in the supermarket. I recommend drinking at least six to eight glasses of water every day. Your skin will look better and your kidneys will be flushed of impurities that may otherwise build up and cause problems for this vital organ.

Vitality Cocktail

Each serving contains 171 calories, 2 mg cholesterol, 2 g fat, and 75 mg sodium

1/2 cup freshly squeezed orange juice
1/2 cup nonfat milk
1 tablespoon each wheat germ, unprocessed wheat bran, and brewer's yeast
1 teaspoon sugar
1/4 teaspoon vanilla extract
4 ice cubes, crushed

This delicious high-protein, high-fiber, low-calorie, low-sodium beverage is an easy, fast, nutritious way to start the day. Add fruits, such as peaches, bananas, and apples, as desired.

Place all ingredients in a blender and blend until smooth.

Makes one 1 1/2-cup serving

Counterfeit Cocktail

Each serving contains negligible calories, no cholesterol, no fat, and 50 mg sodium

Ice cubes, for glass (optional)
Low-sodium soda water
Fresh lime juice, to taste (optional)
Angostura bitters, to taste

Most bars and cocktail lounges have all the ingredients for this delightfully refreshing drink, so you can order it when you are dining out as well as prepare it in your own home. Its decided advantages over most other nonalcoholic drinks are its lack of sweetness, negligible calories, and low sodium content. You can also make it with your favorite sparkling water.

Place ice cubes (if used) in an 8-ounce wine glass, highball glass, or beer mug. Fill glass with soda water, then add lime juice (if used) and enough bitters to tint the drink pale pink.

Makes one 8-ounce serving

Calorie Counter's Wine

Each serving contains 15 calories, no cholesterol, no fat, and 5 mg sodium

Dry red, white, or rosé wine

I suggest using less expensive, rather than valuable, vintage wine in this recipe. The volume of the wine will be reduced by the volume of its alcohol content. Red wine is best served at room temperature; both white and rosé wines should be served chilled.

Pour wine into a nonaluminum saucepan and bring to a slow boil over low heat. When wine starts to boil, ignite it with a match and allow wine to burn until the flame goes out, thus burning off all the alcohol. *Caution: I suggest holding the lighted match with kitchen tongs that are at least 8 inches long so your hand is not close to the boiling wine when you are igniting it.* Allow wine to cool to room temperature, then store, tightly covered, in the refrigerator.

Divide into 3-ounce servings

Bloody Shame

Each serving contains 78 calories, no cholesterol, negligible fat, and 45 mg sodium

2 tablespoons freshly squeezed
    lime juice
4 teaspoons sugar
1/2 teaspoon freshly ground
    black pepper
1 1/2 cups unsalted vegetable
    juice or tomato juice
4 to 6 drops hot-pepper sauce
Ice cubes, for glasses
Raw zucchini or cucumber
    sticks, for garnish (optional)

This zesty Bloody Mary without the vodka is so much lower in sodium than commercial Bloody Mary mixes that you will be proud to serve it and delighted to drink it!

In a medium pitcher mix together lime juice, sugar, and pepper until sugar is dissolved. Add vegetable juice and hot-pepper sauce; mix well. Pour over ice cubes in glasses and garnish each serving with a zucchini stick (if desired).

Makes about 1²/₃ cups, two 6¹/₂-ounce servings

Bloody Mary
Add 6 tablespoons 80-proof vodka to Bloody Shame before pouring into glasses; mix well. This will add 98 calories and a trace of sodium per serving.

Makes 2 cups, two 8-ounce servings

Hot Diggity Dog

Each serving contains 70 calories, no cholesterol, negligible fat, and 3 mg sodium

2 cups freshly squeezed
  grapefruit juice
1/4 teaspoon sugar, plus sugar
  for dipping glasses
Dash cayenne pepper
1 lemon or lime
Ice cubes, for glasses

Made with freshly squeezed grapefruit juice, this is a perfect drink for brunch. Canned or frozen unsweetened grapefruit juice may be substituted if fresh juice is not available.

In a medium pitcher combine juice, the 1/4 teaspoon sugar, and cayenne; mix thoroughly. Set aside.

Cut lemon into 5 thin slices and rub rims of 4 glasses with 1 slice. Place some sugar on a plate and dip rim of each glass into it, shaking off excess. Slice halfway through each remaining slice of lemon and hook a slice over edge of each glass. Fill each glass with ice cubes, then add juice mixture. Mix and serve.

Makes about 2 cups, four 1/2-cup servings

Salty Dog
Add 6 tablespoons 80-proof vodka after cayenne pepper. This will add 49 calories and a trace of sodium per serving.
Makes 2 1/3 cups, about four 1/2-cup plus servings

Piña Colada

Each serving contains 96 calories, 1 mg cholesterol, negligible fat, and 33 mg sodium

1 cup nonfat milk
2 cups unsweetened pineapple
  juice
1 teaspoon sugar
1 teaspoon vanilla extract
1/2 teaspoon coconut extract
2 ice cubes, crushed, plus ice
  cubes for glasses

This drink is so surprisingly delicious that you will want to serve it on every occasion you can think of. I even serve it as a chilled soup before a curry dinner.

Into a blender, place milk, juice, sugar, extracts, and crushed ice cubes and blend until mixture is smooth and frothy. Pour over ice cubes in 4 chilled glasses.

Makes 3 1/4 cups, four 6 1/2-ounce servings

Fresh Fruit Frappé

Each serving contains 113 calories, 1 mg cholesterol, 1 g fat, and 33 mg sodium

1 medium banana (7 oz),
  peeled and sliced
1 teaspoon freshly squeezed
  lemon juice
1 can (8 oz) crushed pineapple
  in natural juice, undrained
1 cup freshly squeezed orange
  juice
1 cup nonfat milk
1 teaspoon vanilla extract
4 ice cubes, crushed
Mint sprigs, for garnish
  (optional)

Enjoy this tangy combination of ingredients either as a beverage or as a sauce over fresh fruit for dessert. It is a perfect quick-energy boost.

In a blender place banana and lemon juice and blend until smooth. Add pineapple with its juice, orange juice, milk, vanilla, and ice cubes; blend until mixture is smooth and frothy. Pour into 4 chilled glasses and garnish with fresh mint (if desired).

Makes about 4 cups, four 1-cup servings

Desert Tea

Each serving contains 2 calories, no cholesterol, no fat, and 7 mg sodium

2 tea bags
2 quarts cold water

Brewing tea in the heat of the sun makes the best iced tea imaginable. For variety, add freshly grated orange zest or crushed mint leaves to the jar with the tea bags.

Place tea bags in a 2-quart glass jar or bottle with a lid, fill container with the water, and cover. Place in the sun until tea is desired strength (2 hours or more, depending on intensity of sun). Remove tea bags; serve tea over ice or chill it in the refrigerator.

Makes 2 quarts, eight 1-cup servings

Low-Sodium Peanut Butter Punch

Each serving contains 168 calories, 2 mg cholesterol, 8 g fat, and 66 mg sodium

1 cup nonfat milk
2 tablespoons creamy unsalted
    peanut butter
1 tablespoon date sugar or 2
    dates, pitted and chopped
1 teaspoon vanilla extract
4 ice cubes, crushed
Ground cinnamon or nutmeg,
    for sprinkling (optional)

For all of you who share my addiction to peanut butter, I have come up with a way you can drink it in a delicious and unusual beverage that is not only high in protein but also low in sodium.

Into a blender container place milk, peanut butter, sugar, vanilla, and ice cubes and blend until smooth and creamy. Pour mixture into 2 chilled glasses and sprinkle each serving with a little cinnamon (if desired).

Makes about 1²/₃ cups, two 6¹/₂-ounce servings

Hot Peanut Butter Punch
Omit ice cubes and serve hot for breakfast instead of cocoa.

High-Potassium Punch

Each serving contains 135 calories, 2 mg cholesterol, 1 g fat, and 64 mg sodium

¹/₂ cup chopped pitted dates
1 medium banana (7 oz),
    peeled and sliced
2 cups nonfat milk
1 teaspoon vanilla extract
4 ice cubes, crushed
Ground cinnamon or nutmeg,
    for sprinkling (optional)

Two ingredients in this beverage are naturally high in potassium—bananas and dates. Combining them in one drink gives you a tasty, power-packed beverage.

Into a blender container place all ingredients and blend until mixture is smooth and creamy. Pour into 4 chilled glasses and sprinkle a little cinnamon on each serving (if desired).

Makes about 4 cups, four 1-cup servings

The following suggestions may prove helpful for low-sodium cooking as well as general cooking and menu planning.

Cholesterol

To lower the amount of cholesterol in your diet, apply the following restrictions:

- Limit shellfish, such as oysters, clams, scallops, lobster, shrimp, and crab.

- Limit or avoid egg yolks.

- Limit or avoid organ meats, such as liver, heart, kidneys, sweetbreads, and brains.

Commercial Condiments

This book includes recipes for practically all the condiments and sauces available commercially in low-sodium form, such as relish, mayonnaise, and salad dressings, because many commercial low-sodium products are expensive, not widely available, and not very tasty. Anyone on a sodium-restricted diet can become independent enough within the prescribed diet program to create basic condiments in the kitchen.

Eggs

When raw eggs or raw egg whites will be consumed in a prepared dish, it is important to coddle the egg by dipping the whole egg in the shell in boiling water for 30 seconds before using it. The avidin, a component of raw egg whites, is believed to block the absorption of biotin, one of the water-soluble vitamins. Coddling the egg inactivates the avidin, which is extremely sensitive to heat. (Coddling does not destroy salmonella bacteria, however.)

Fructose

For those desiring to reduce their caloric intake from sugar, fructose is a good alternative sweetener. This natural fruit sugar, found in most supermarkets, is about one and a half times sweeter than ordinary table sugar (sucrose). Because less is needed in a given dish, the caloric content is reduced. I have found fructose to be the best flavor heightener in vegetable preparations where salt is not used. I also routinely use it in small amounts in marinades, even when the overall desired effect is not sweetness, because fructose sharpens the taste of the other ingredients.

Low-Sodium Baking Powder

Regular baking powder contains 40 milligrams of sodium per teaspoon, whereas low-sodium baking powder contains only 1 milligram per teaspoon. When using the latter, however, you will need to add half again as much (50 percent more) as you would if using regular baking powder. Low-sodium baking powder is available in many health-food stores, or you can ask your druggist to make it for you according to the following formula.

Cornstarch: 56.0 grams
Potassium bitartrate: 112.25 grams
Potassium bicarbonate: 79.5 grams
Tartaric acid: 15.0 grams

Saturated Fat

To lower the amount of saturated fat in your diet, apply the following rules:

- Instead of butter, use margarine and liquid vegetable oils that are high in unsaturated fats, such as extra virgin olive oil and corn oil.

- Do not use tropical oils, such as coconut oil and palm oil, or solid chocolate. Many nondairy creamers and sour cream substitutes contain coconut oil, and hard chocolate contains cocoa butter. Use coconut extract and dry powdered cocoa for flavor instead.

- Use nonfat milk.

- Avoid commercial ice cream that is high in saturated fat.

- Have beef, lamb, and pork no more than four or five times a week. Eat fish and the white meat of chicken and turkey (without skin) instead.

- Buy lean cuts of meat and remove all visible fat before cooking.

- Avoid processed meats and high-fat cheeses.

Smoke Flavoring

Sold as a liquid in supermarkets, smoke flavoring is a boon to a low-sodium diet because it adds the smoky flavor usually associated with high-sodium ingredients without adding any sodium and very few calories.

Wines

When using wine for cooking, avoid wines labeled "cooking wine" because they contain salt. In fact, the term *cooking wine* comes from a time when wine for kitchen use was salted to prevent the cook from drinking it.

Kitchen Vocabulary

Bake To cook in a heated oven.

Barbecue To roast or broil over hot coals.

Baste To spoon liquid over food while it is cooking (a baster can also be used).

Beat To mix, in order to add air and increase volume, with an egg beater or electric mixer or by hand, stirring rapidly in a circular motion.

Beat stiffly To whip until mixture stands in stiff peaks.

Blanch To dip quickly into boiling water. Usually refers to fruits and vegetables. When blanching nuts, cover shelled nuts with cold water and bring to a boil. Remove from heat and drain. Slip skins from nuts.

Blend To combine two or more ingredients until well mixed; often used when referring to an electric blender.

Blend until frothy To blend until the substance is foamy and the volume is almost doubled by the addition of air.

Boil   To heat liquid to the boiling point (212° F at sea level), or cook food in hot liquid in which bubbles constantly rise to the surface and break.

Bone   To remove all bones; usually refers to roasts and poultry.

Braise   To brown meat well on all sides, adding a small amount of water or other liquid, then cover and simmer over low heat or place in a moderate oven and cook until tender or as recipe directs.

Broil   To cook under broiler at designated distance from heat.

Brown   To cook to desired color in the oven, under a broiler, or in a heavy skillet.

Brunoise   A mixture of vegetables that are finely diced.

Chill   To place in refrigerator until cold.

Chop   To use one hand to hold a large chopping knife, pointed end down, on cutting surface and other hand to guide food being chopped. Cleavers and other alternatives to knives are available in most appliance and hardware stores.

Coarsely chop   To chop in pieces approximately 1/2 inch square.

Coat   With a sifter, to sprinkle food with flour, sugar, or other ingredient until coated, or to roll in dry ingredient or shake in a paper bag until coated.

Coddle   Usually refers to eggs. When a raw egg is called for in a dish that will not be cooked, place the whole egg in boiling water for 30 seconds before using it. Coddling inactivates the avidin, an extremely heat-sensitive component of raw egg white believed to block the absorption of biotin, a water-soluble vitamin.

Cool   To allow to stand at room temperature until no longer warm to the touch.

Core   To remove central part, usually from fruits such as pears and apples.

Cover tightly   To seal so that steam cannot escape.

Cream   To beat a mixture of ingredients with a spoon or an electric mixer until soft, smooth, and well mixed.

Crumble   To crush ingredient into crumbs with your hands or a fork.

Crush   To grind ingredients such as dried herbs with a mortar and pestle.

Cube   To cut ingredient into cube-shaped pieces approximately 1 inch square or size specified in recipe.

Deep-fry   To cook food in a deep-fat fryer in enough oil to cover. If temperature is given in the recipe, a deep-fat thermometer is needed.

Dice To cut into ¼-inch cubes or smaller.

Dissolve To mix dry ingredients with liquid until no longer visible in the solution.

Dot To scatter or sprinkle small bits of ingredient, usually butter or margarine, over surface of food.

Dredge To coat with flour.

Fillet To remove all bones; usually refers to fish.

Finely chop To cut into small pieces.

Fold in To move a rubber spatula or spoon in a circular motion across the bottom of a mixture in a bowl and up over the surface, repeating until ingredients are blended.

Fork-tender When food can be easily pierced with a fork.

Fry To cook in a small amount of oil in a skillet.

Grate To rub the surface of a solid food against an abrasive object, such as a grater, to produce particles of a desired size.

Grease To rub lightly with margarine, corn oil, or other lubricant.

Grind To pulverize food with a chopper or grinder.

Julienne To cut into strips approximately ⅛ inch by 2 inches.

Knead To work dough with hands by pressing and folding until smooth and satiny; usually refers to bread dough.

Marinate To allow food to stand in a savory liquid, usually to enrich flavor or tenderize, for length of time indicated in recipe.

Mash To crush ingredient to a soft, pulpy mass with a potato masher, electric blender, or mixer.

Mince To chop very finely.

Pan-broil To cook in hot, ungreased or cured skillet, pouring off fat as it accumulates.

Parboil To boil in water or other liquid until partially cooked. Usually precedes another form of cooking.

Pare To remove the relatively thin outer covering of such food as apples and peaches with a knife.

Peel To remove the thick rind of food such as oranges and bananas, and the outer covering of shrimp.

Pit To remove the seed from such fruits as peaches and plums.

Poach To gently cook for a short time in simmering liquid.

Preheat To allow oven to reach desired temperature before baking.

Press This term usually applies to garlic when using a garlic press. Garlic does not have to be peeled before it is placed in a press, so this is a popular method of adding fresh garlic to recipes.

Purée To process food through a fine sieve or food mill, or in an electric blender or food processor to achieve a soft, smooth consistency.

Roast To bake meat or poultry.

Sauté To cook, in a skillet, in just enough hot liquid to prevent scorching.

Scald To heat to just below the boiling point, when tiny bubbles start to form at sides of pan. Also referred to as bringing just to the boiling point.

Score To make shallow cuts or slits on the surface of food with a knife.

Scrape To remove, with an edged instrument, the outer skin of food such as carrots and parsnips, or abrade food such as onions to produce juice.

Sear To brown surface rapidly over high heat in a hot skillet.

Seed To completely remove small seeds from such foods as tomatoes, cucumbers, and bell peppers.

Shred With a knife, to slice ingredient thinly in two directions, or to use a shredder to achieve some texture.

Sift To process dry ingredients such as flour and sugar through a flour sifter or sieve to blend ingredients and reduce large particles to smaller ones.

Simmer To cook just below boiling point (about 185° F at sea level).

Singe To hold over flame to burn off all hairs. Usually refers to poultry.

Skewer To spear chunks of food on wooden or metal skewers, such as for shish kabob.

Skin To remove skin of such foods as chicken and fish.

Slice To cut food to specified thickness with a sharp knife.

Snip To cut into small pieces using scissors or kitchen shears.

Sprinkle To scatter drops or particles of food as directed in recipe.

Steam   To cook food over boiling water in a steamer or large kettle, with a rack placed in the bottom of container to hold food above the boiling water.

Steep   To allow to stand in hot liquid.

Stiff but not dry   Usually used to describe beaten egg whites; they should hold soft, well-defined peaks but not be beaten to brittleness.

Stir   To mix ingredients with a spoon moved in a slow, circular motion.

Thicken   To mix thickening agent, such as arrowroot, cornstarch, or flour, first with only a small amount of the hot liquid to be thickened, then slowly add mixture to the remaining hot liquid, stirring constantly. Mixture should be cooked until it coats a metal spoon. Puréed vegetables and fruits can also be used to thicken soups and sauces.

Thinly slice   To use a knife or the thin-slicing side of a four-sided grater to cut vegetables such as cucumbers and onions.

Toast   To brown in a toaster, oven, or under a broiler. When applied to nuts, seeds, or coconut, cook to desired color in 350° F oven, place under broiler, or cook in skillet on top of stove; watch carefully, since nuts burn easily.

Toss   To mix food from both sides of bowl or container in an under-and-over motion toward the center, using two spoons or a fork and spoon; usually refers to salads.

Whip   To beat rapidly with a fork, whisk, egg beater, or electric mixer to add air and increase volume of mixture.

Whisk   To stir, beat, or fold using a wire whisk.

Zest   Pigmented, thin outer skin of an orange or lemon, used as flavoring.

Sodium and Calorie Guide

This list will help you keep track of sodium and calories when you plan meals. It is not meant to be complete, and the numbers are approximate, since both the sodium and caloric content of foods varies according to natural occurrences, such as where on the tree a fruit developed, what ocean a fish lived in, or how much rainfall a plant received. Processing also contributes to variations in nutrient levels, since handling and packaging vary among producers.

I have purposely not included most packaged and processed foods on this list because the calorie and sodium figures per serving are almost always available on the product label. Since different brands may have slightly different ingredients, it is best if you simply cultivate the habit of reading labels very carefully to familiarize yourself with the products you most often use. You cannot always trust buzzwords such as low-sodium or sodium-reduced, so read the actual figures in the fine print to learn if the product is indeed low enough in sodium to suit your diet.

Fortunately, since I first wrote this book about 10 years ago, many new low-sodium products have been introduced in the marketplace, and many items are now available without added sodium. Since sodium is a naturally occurring ingredient in all foods, however, this list will give you a better understanding of just how much sodium you can consume even without using your saltshaker and how calories can add up even without added fats and sugars.

	Sodium (in mg.)	Calories
Beverage		
Beer and Wine		
Ale, mild (8 oz)	17	98
Beer (8 oz)	8	114
Champagne, brut (3 oz)	3	75
Champagne, extra dry (3 oz)	3	87
Dubonnet (3 oz)	4	96
Marsala, dry (3 oz)	4	162
Marsala, sweet (3 oz)	4	152
Muscatel (4 oz)	4	158
Port (4 oz)	4	158
Red Wine, dry (3 oz)	4	69
Sake (3 oz)	4	75
Sherry, dry (3.5 oz)	10	115
Sherry, sweet (3.5 oz)	13	135
Vermouth, dry (3.5 oz)	4	105
Vermouth, sweet (3.5 oz)	4	167
White wine, dry (3 oz)	4	74
Liqueurs and Cordials		
Amaretto (1 oz)	2	112
Crème de menthe (1 oz)	2	101
Curaçao (1 oz)	2	112
Drambuie (1 oz)	2	100
Tía María (1 oz)	2	113
Spirits (bourbon, brandy, Canadian whiskey, Cognac, gin, rum, rye, Scotch whisky, tequila, and vodka—calories depend on the proof)		
80 proof (1 oz)	trace	67

	Sodium (in mg.)	Calories
80 proof (1 oz)	trace	67
84 proof (1 oz)	trace	70
90 proof (1 oz)	trace	75
94 proof (1 oz)	trace	78
97 proof (1 oz)	trace	81
100 proof (1 oz)	trace	83
Coffee and Tea		
Coffee, brewed, 1 cup	5	5
Coffee, instant, 1 cup	1	2
Tea, brewed, 1 cup	7	2

Eggs

	Sodium (in mg.)	Calories
1 large white, raw	75	24
1 large yolk, raw	12	94
Egg Substitute (see page 76)	58	62

Fish and Shellfish
(3 oz raw, not processed)

	Sodium (in mg.)	Calories
Abalone	217	83
Anchovy	87	109
Bass	58	79
Catfish	51	88
Caviar	1,871	223
Clams	31	70
Cod	59	66
Crab	619	125
Flounder	66	67
Halibut	46	85
Herring	57	199
Lobster	179	78
Oysters	62	77
Perch, Atlantic	67	75
Perch, Pacific	54	81
Red snapper	57	79
Salmon, Atlantic	63	185
Salmon, chinook	38	189

	Sodium (in mg.)	Calories
Salmon, coho	41	158
Scallops	217	69
Shrimp	119	77
Sole	66	67
Swordfish	46	100
Trout, brook	40	86
Trout, rainbow	69	166
Tuna, albacore	34	150
Tuna, yellowfin	31	113
Yellowtail	63	117

Fruits, dried (1 oz)

	Sodium (in mg.)	Calories
Apples	25	69
Apricots	3	67
Dates	1	78
Figs	3	72
Pears	2	74
Prunes, pitted	1	68
Raisins, seedless	3	85

Fruits, fresh

	Sodium (in mg.)	Calories
Apples, 1 medium	0	81
Apricots, 1 medium	*	17
Avocados, 1/2 medium	10	153
Bananas, 1 medium	1	105
Blackberries, 1/2 cup	0	38
Blueberries, 1/2 cup	4	41
Cherries, sour, 1 cup pitted	3	52
Cranberries, 1 cup	1	47
Figs, 1 medium	1	47
Grapefruit, 1/2 medium	0	39
Grapes, 1 cup	2	59
Guavas, 1 medium	3	46
Kumquats, 1 medium	1	12
Lemons, 1 medium	1	17
Limes, 1 medium	1	20

* Negligible

171

	Sodium (in mg.)	Calories
Mangos, 1 medium	4	135
Melons		
Canteloupe, 1/2 medium	24	93
Honeydew, 1/2 medium	7	23
Watermelon, cubed, 1 cup	3	52
Nectarines, 1 medium	0	67
Oranges, 1 medium	0	62
Papayas, 1 medium	9	119
Peaches, 1 medium	0	37
Pears, 1 medium	0	98
Persimmons		
Japanese, 1 medium	2	118
Native, 1 medium	*	32
Pineapples, chopped, 1 cup	2	77
Plums, 1 medium	0	36
Pomegranates, 1 medium	5	105
Raspberries, 1/2 cup	0	31
Rhubarb, chopped and cooked, 1/2 cup	3	13
Strawberries, 1/2 cup	1	23
Tangerines, 1 medium	1	37

Herbs, Spices, Seasonings, and Gelatin
(1 teaspoon, dried, unless otherwise noted)

	Sodium (in mg.)	Calories
Allspice, ground	2	5
Anise seed	*	8
Basil	1	4
Bay leaf	*	2
Caraway seed	*	8
Celery seed	4	9
Chili powder	26	8
Cinnamon, ground	1	6
Cloves, ground	5	7
Coriander seed	1	2
Cumin seed	3	8

	Sodium (in mg.)	Calories
Curry powder	1	7
Dill weed	2	3
Fennel seed	2	7
Garlic powder	1	9
Gelatin, powdered, unflavored (1 envelope)	6	23
Ginger, ground	1	6
Hot-pepper sauce	22	*
Mace, ground	1	9
Marjoram	*	2
Mustard seed	*	18
Nutmeg, ground	*	12
Onion powder	1	8
Oregano	*	5
Paprika	1	7
Parsley	2	1
Pepper, ground		
Black	1	6
Cayenne	7	6
White	*	7
Poultry seasoning	*	4
Rosemary	1	4
Saffron	1	2
Sage	*	2
Salt	2,208	0
Smoke flavoring	0	1
Sugar	*	16
Summer savory	*	4
Tarragon	1	5
Thyme	1	4
Turmeric, ground	1	8
Vanilla extract	0	14
Vinegar	*	1

Negligible

	Sodium (in mg.)	Calories		Sodium (in mg.)	Calories
Meats and Poultry			Ham, fresh, lean part		
(3 oz raw, unprocessed, unless noted)			only, cooked	61	189
Beef			Leg	47	116
Brains	88	107	Loin	54	51
Chuck	65	110	Sirloin	37	235
Flank	60	167	Spareribs	65	243
Heart	73	92	Tenderloin	42	95
Kidney	53	110	Quail	43	60
Liver	62	122	Rabbit	37	138
Porterhouse	47	133	Squab	43	121
Rib roast	45	61	Turkey, meat only		
Round steak	44	114	Breast	51	99
Rump	64	55	Dark meat, roasted	67	159
Sirloin	44	221	White meat, roasted	54	133
T-bone	47	135	Veal		
Tongue	62	176	Breast	55	197
Tripe	61	85	Chuck	58	147
Chicken, meat only			Flank	49	267
Breast	58	99	Loin	57	154
Dark meat, roasted	79	174	Round	58	139
Liver	67	106	Venison	77	107
White meat, roasted	43	130			
Duck, meat only	63	112			
Frog's legs	47	62	**Nuts, unsalted (¹/₄ cup)**		
Goose, meat only	74	137	Almonds, raw	4	202
Lamb			Brazil nuts, raw	1	230
Leg	50	223	Cashews, dry roasted	6	199
Loin	49	249	Coconut, dried	4	72
Rib	47	265	Hazelnuts, raw	1	182
Shoulder	55	134	Macadamia nuts, dry roasted	2	238
Pheasant	32	113	Peanuts, dry roasted	6	207
Pork			Pecans, raw	*	183
Bacon	621	473	Pine nuts, raw	2	206
Blade	60	140	Pistachio nuts, dry roasted	2	187
Canadian bacon	1,197	133	Walnuts, raw	*	192
Ham, cured, canned	837	142			

* Negligible

	Sodium (in mg.)	Calories		Sodium (in mg.)	Calories
Seeds (¹/₄ cup)			Endive	6	4
Poppy seeds	8	190	Eggplant	2	11
Pumpkin seeds	6	189	Garlic, 1 clove	1	5
Sesame seeds	15	215	Ginger	6	34
Sunflower seeds	1	208	Leeks	11	32
			Lettuce	2	4
Vegetables, (¹/₂ cup, cooked) dried			Mushrooms	1	9
Chick-peas, canned	300	120	Onions	2	28
Great Northern beans	2	108	Parsley	12	10
Kidney beans	2	119	Parsnips	7	51
Lentils	13	106	Peas, edible-pod	4	60
Lima beans	3	115	Peas, green	3	30
Navy beans	1	94	Potatoes, 1 medium, baked	16	220
Split peas	12	104	Pumpkins	1	15
			Radishes	14	10
Vegetables, fresh (¹/₂ cup raw, unless noted)			Rutabagas	14	26
Alfalfa sprouts	1	5	Shallots	10	58
Artichoke, 1 medium,			Spinach	22	6
steamed	79	53	Squash		
Asparagus	1	15	Acorn	2	28
Beans, green	3	17	Butternut	3	32
Beets	49	30	Hubbard	4	24
Bell peppers	2	13	Spaghetti	9	17
Broccoli	12	12	Summer	1	13
Brussels sprouts	11	19	Sweet potatoes	9	71
Cabbage	14	18	Tomatoes	4	9
Carrots	20	24	Turnips	44	18
Cauliflower	8	12	Water chestnuts	8	67
Celeriac	79	31	Watercress	7	2
Celery	54	10	Yams	7	90
Chiles	5	30	Zucchini	1	13
Chives	2	6			
Corn	12	66			
Cucumbers	1	7			

Beverages

Coffee

  Noninstant ground 1 pound,
    80 tablespoons = 40 to 50 cups brewed

  Instant 4-ounce jar = 60 cups brewed

Ice cubes 2 = $^1/_4$ cup melted

Tea 1 ounce = 20 cups brewed

Cereals and Grain Products

Bread crumbs

  Dry 2 slices = $^1/_2$ cup crumbled; 4 slices = $^1/_2$ cup
    finely ground

  Soft 1 slice = $^3/_4$ cup

Bulgur $^1/_3$ cup = 1 cup cooked

Cornmeal 1 cup = 4 cups cooked

Flour

  All-purpose 1 pound = 4 cups

  Cake 1 pound = 4 $^1/_2$ cups sifted

  Whole wheat 1 pound = 4 cups

Graham crackers 14 squares = 1 cup finely crumbled

Oatmeal 1 cup = 2 cups cooked

Rice

  Brown 1 pound, 2 $^1/_2$ cups = 7 $^1/_2$ cups cooked

  White 1 pound, 2 $^1/_2$ cups = 5 cups cooked

  Wild 5 $^1/_2$ ounces, 1 cup = 3$^1/_2$ to 4 cups cooked

Soda crackers 21 squares = 1 cup finely crumbled

Cheese

American $^1/_4$ pound = 1 cup grated

Blue 5 ounces = 1 cup crumbled

Cheddar $^1/_4$ pound = 1 cup grated

Cottage cheese, not packed

  Dry curd 5 $^1/_2$ ounces = 1 cup

  Large curd 8 ounces = 1 cup

  Small curd 7 $^1/_2$ ounces = 1 cup

Cream cheese 3-ounce package = 6 tablespoons

Monterey jack $^1/_4$ pound = 1 cup grated

Parmesan 3 $^1/_2$ ounces = 1 cup grated; 3 ounces =
  1 cup shredded

Ricotta, whole or low-fat 8 ounces = 1 cup

Swiss $^1/_4$ pound = 1 cup grated

Eggs

Eggs, raw

  Whole 6 medium = 1 cup

  White 1 medium = 1 $^1/_2$ tablespoons; 8 medium =
    1 cup

  Yolk 1 medium = 1 tablespoon; 16 medium =
    1 cup

Hard-cooked 1 medium = $^1/_3$ cup finely chopped

Egg substitute, liquid $^1/_2$ cup = 2 eggs (see page 76)

Fish and Shellfish

Anchovies 3 fillets, drained and chopped = 1 teaspoon

Crab $^1/_2$ pound, fresh, frozen, cooked, or canned =
  1 cup

Lobster $^1/_2$ pound, fresh or frozen, cooked = 1 cup

Oysters $^1/_2$ pound, raw = 1 cup

Scallops $^1/_2$ pound, fresh or frozen = 1 cup

Shrimp 1 pound, shelled and cooked = 3 cups

Tuna 6- to 7 $^1/_2$-ounce can, drained = $^3/_4$ cup

Fruits, dried

Apples 1 pound = 8 cups diced

Apricots 1 pound = 8 cups diced

Dates 1 pound whole, 2 $^1/_2$ cups = 1 $^3/_4$ cups pitted
  and chopped

Figs 1 pound, 2 $^1/_2$ cups = 4 $^1/_2$ cups cooked; 2 cups
  chopped

Pears 1 pound, 3 cups = 5$^1/_2$ cups cooked

Prunes, pitted 1 pound, 2 $^1/_2$ cups = 3 $^3/_4$ cups cooked

Raisins, seedless 1 pound, 2 $^3/_4$ cups = 3 $^3/_4$ cups
  cooked; 2 cups chopped

Fruits, fresh

Apples 1 $^1/_2$ pounds, 6 small = 4 cups sliced;
  4 $^1/_2$ cups chopped

Apricots   1 pound, 6 to 8 average = 2 cups chopped
Avocados   1 medium = 2 cups chopped
Bananas   1 pound, 4 small = 2 cups mashed
Blueberries   1 pint = 2 cups
Cherries   2 cups = 1 cup pitted
Cranberries   1 pound = 4 $\frac{1}{2}$ cups whole; 4 cups chopped
Figs   1 pound, 4 small = 2 cups chopped
Grapefruit   1 small = 1 cup sectioned
Grapes
   Concord $\frac{1}{4}$ pound, 30 grapes = 1 cup
   Thompson seedless $\frac{1}{4}$ pound, 40 grapes = 1 cup
Guavas   1 pound, 4 medium = 1 cup
Kumquats   1 pound, 8 to 10 average = 2 cups sliced
Lemons $\frac{1}{4}$ pound, 1 medium = 3 tablespoons juice; 2 teaspoons grated zest
Limes $\frac{1}{2}$ pound, 5 average = 4 tablespoons juice; 4 to 5 teaspoons grated zest
Loquats   1 pound, 5 average = 1 $\frac{1}{2}$ cups chopped
Lychees   1 pound, 6 average = $\frac{1}{2}$ cup chopped
Mangoes   1 pound, 2 average = 1 $\frac{1}{2}$ cups chopped
Melons
   Cantaloupe   2 pounds, 1 average = 3 cups diced
   Crenshaw   3 pounds, 1 average = 4 $\frac{1}{2}$ cups diced
   Honeydew   2 pounds, 1 average = 3 cups diced
   Watermelon   10 to 12 pounds, 1 average = 20 to 24 cups cubed
Nectarines   1 pound, 3 average = 2 cups chopped
Oranges   1 pound, 3 average = 1 cup juice; 3 cups sections
Papayas   1 pound = 2 cups cubed, 1 cup puréed
Peaches   1 pound, 3 average = 2 cups chopped
Pears   1 pound, 3 average = 2 cups chopped
Persimmons   1 pound, 3 average = 2 cups mashed
Pineapple   3 pounds, 1 medium = 2 $\frac{1}{2}$ cups chopped
Plums   1 pound, 4 average = 2 cups chopped
Pomegranates $\frac{1}{4}$ pound, 1 average = 3 cups seeds
Raspberries   4 $\frac{1}{2}$ ounces = 1 cup
Rhubarb   1 pound, 4 stalks = 2 cups chopped and cooked

Strawberries   5 ounces = 1 cup
Tangerines   1 pound, 4 average = 2 cups sections

Herbs, Spices, Seasonings, and Gelatin
Garlic powder $\frac{1}{4}$ teaspoon = 2 small cloves fresh garlic
Gelatin, powdered   1 envelope = 1 scant tablespoon
Ginger, ground $\frac{1}{2}$ teaspoon = 1 teaspoon grated fresh ginger
Herbs, dried $\frac{1}{2}$ teaspoon crushed = 1 tablespoon fresh
Horseradish, bottled   2 tablespoons = 1 tablespoon fresh

Meats and Poultry
Bacon   1 slice, cooked = 1 tablespoon crumbled
Chicken   3 $\frac{1}{2}$ pounds, roasted, boned, and skinned = 3 cups chopped
Escargot   6 = 1 $\frac{1}{2}$ ounces
Meat   1 pound, raw, cubed or chopped = 2 cups tightly packed

Milk and Milk Products, Except Cheese
Butter and margarine $\frac{1}{4}$ pound, 1 cube = $\frac{1}{2}$ cup (8 tablespoons)
Cream, whipping   1 cup = 2 cups whipped
Evaporated skimmed, canned   1 cup = 5 cups whipped
Powdered milk
   Buttermilk, powdered   3 tablespoons + 1 cup water = 1 cup buttermilk
   Instant nonfat $\frac{1}{3}$ cup + $\frac{2}{3}$ cup water = 1 cup nonfat milk
   Noninstant nonfat   3 tablespoons + 1 cup water = 1 cup nonfat milk
   Whole $\frac{1}{4}$ cup + 1 cup water = 1 cup whole milk

Nuts
Almonds   32 whole = $\frac{1}{4}$ cup chopped; 8 whole = 1 tablespoon chopped
Brazil nuts $\frac{1}{2}$ pound = 1 $\frac{1}{2}$ cups
Coconut $\frac{1}{2}$ pound shredded = 2 $\frac{1}{2}$ cups

Macadamia nuts   3 whole = 1 tablespoon finely
   chopped
Peanuts   44 whole = $^1/_4$ cup chopped; 11 whole =
   1 tablespoon chopped
Pecans   20 halves = $^1/_4$ cup chopped; 5 halves =
   1 tablespoon chopped
Walnuts   12 halves = $^1/_4$ cup chopped; 3 halves =
   1 tablespoon chopped

Pasta, Dried

Asian noodles (thin) $^3/_4$ pound dry = 5 cups cooked
Linguine   8 ounces = 4 cups cooked
Macaroni   1 pound, 5 cups = 12 cups cooked
Rotelle pasta   1 pound, 4 cups = 6 cups cooked
Rotini pasta $^1/_2$ pound, 3 cups = 4 cups cooked
Spaghetti   8 ounces = 4 cups cooked

Vegetables, Dried

Chick-peas   1 pound, 2 cups dry = 6 cups cooked
Kidney beans   1 pound, 1 $^1/_2$ cups dry = 4 cups cooked
Lentils   1 cup dry = 2 cups cooked
Lima, navy, or pinto beans   1 pound, 2 $^1/_2$ cups dry =
   6 cups cooked
Split peas   1 pound, 2 cups dry = 5 cups cooked

Vegetables, Fresh

Artichokes $^1/_2$ pound = 1 average
Arugula $^1/_2$ pound = 2 cups bite-sized pieces
Asparagus   1 pound, 18 spears = 2 cups 1-inch pieces
Beans, green   1 pound = 5 cups 1-inch pieces
Beets   1 pound, 5 average = 6 cups sliced; 2 $^1/_2$ cups
   cooked
Bell peppers   1 pound, 3 medium = 2 cups seeded and
   finely chopped; 4 cups sliced
Broccoli   1 pound, 2 stalks = 6 cups chopped and
   cooked
Brussels sprouts   1 pound, 28 average = 4 cups
Cabbage   1 pound = 4 cups shredded; 2 $^1/_2$ cups
   cooked

Carrots   1 pound, 6 medium = 4 cups grated; 3 cups
   sliced
Cauliflower   1 $^1/_2$ pounds, 1 average head = 6 cups
   chopped and cooked
Celery $^1/_2$ pound = 1 $^1/_2$ cups chopped; 1 stalk =
   $^1/_2$ cup finely chopped
Celery root   1 $^3/_4$ pounds, 1 average = 4 cups grated;
   2 cups cooked mashed
Chiles, jalapeño $^1/_2$ pound, 16 chiles = 2 cups chopped
Corn   6 ears = 2 $^1/_2$ cups cut, whole kernels; 2 cups
   scraped flesh and liquid
Cucumbers $^1/_2$ pound, 1 medium = 1 $^1/_2$ cups sliced;
   1 cup diced
Eggplant   1 pound, 1 medium = twelve $^1/_4$-inch slices;
   6 cups cubed
Garlic   1 clove = 1 teaspoon finely chopped
Leeks   1 pound = $^1/_2$ pound, white part only = 2 cups
   chopped; 1 cup cooked
Lettuce   1 $^1/_2$ pounds, 1 average head = 6 cups bite-
   sized pieces
Mushrooms $^1/_2$ pound = 2 cups sliced
Onions
   Boiling   1 pound = 16
   Full size $^1/_2$ pound, 1 medium = 1 $^1/_2$ cups finely
      chopped
   Green   4-ounce bunch, 6 average = 1 cup chopped
   Pearl   10 ounces = 2 cups
Parsley   1 pound = 8 cups tightly packed, 8 cups finely
   chopped; 2 ounces = 1 cup tightly packed, 1 cup
   finely chopped
Parsnips   1 pound, 6 average = 4 cups chopped
Potatoes   1 pound, 2 medium = 3 cups coarsely
   chopped; 2 $^1/_2$ cups cooked and diced
Pumpkins   3 pounds, 1 average = 4 cups cooked and
   mashed
Radicchio   10 ounces, 1 average head = 2 $^1/_2$ cups bite-
   sized pieces
Rutabagas   1 $^1/_2$ pounds, 3 small = 2 cups cooked and
   mashed
Shallots $^1/_4$ pound = $^1/_4$ cup chopped

Spinach   1 pound = 4 cups bite-sized pieces; $1^1/_2$ cups
   cooked

Squash

   Acorn $1^1/_2$ pounds, 1 average = 2 cups cooked and
      mashed

   Banana   3 pounds, 1 average = 4 cups cooked and
      mashed

   Chayote $^1/_2$ pound, 1 average = $^1/_2$ cup diced;
      $^3/_4$ cup sliced

   Spaghetti   5 pounds, 1 medium = 8 cups cooked

   Summer   1 pound, 4 average = 1 cup cooked

   Zucchini 1 pound, 2 average = 3 cups diced; 4 cups
      thinly sliced; $1^1/_2$ cups cooked and chopped

Tomatillos $^1/_4$ pound, 4 small = 1 cup chopped

Tomatoes 1 pound, 3 medium = 2 cups peeled, seeded,
   and chopped; $1^1/_4$ cups cooked and chopped

Turnips   1 pound = 2 cups peeled and grated; 4 cups
   bite-sized pieces; $1^1/_4$ cups cooked and mashed

Watercress $^1/_4$ pound, 1 bunch = 1 cup loosely packed

U.S. Measure and Metric Measure Conversion Chart
Formulas for Exact Measures

Measure	Symbol	When You Know	Multiply by	To Find
Mass (weight)	oz	ounces	28.35	grams
	lb	pounds	0.45	kilograms
	g	grams	0.035	ounces
	kg	kilograms	2.2	pounds
Volume	tsp	teaspoons	4.9	milliliters
	tbsp	tablespoons	15.0	milliliters
	fl oz	fluid ounces	29.57	milliliters
	c	cups	0.237	liters
	pt	pints	0.47	liters
	qt	quarts	0.95	liters
	gal	gallons	3.785	liters
	ml	milliliters	0.034	fluid ounces
Temperature	°F	Fahrenheit	$5/9$ (after subtracting 32)	Celsius
	°C	Celsius	$9/5$ (then add 32)	Fahrenheit

Rounded Measures for Quick Reference

Mass (weight)	1 oz		= 30 g
	4 oz		= 115 g
	8 oz		= 225 g
	16 oz	= 1 lb	= 450 g
	32 oz	= 2 lb	= 900 g
	36 oz	= 2 1/4 lb	1,000 g (1 kg)
Volume	1/4 tsp	= 1/24 oz	= 1 ml
	1/2 tsp	= 1/12 oz	= 2 ml
	1 tsp	= 1/6 oz	= 5 ml
	1 tbsp	= 1/2 oz	= 15 ml
	1 c	= 8 oz	= 250 ml
	2 c (1 pt)	= 16 oz	= 500 ml
	4 c (1 qt)	= 32 oz	= 1 liter
	4 qt (1 gal)	= 128 oz	3 3/4 liter
Temperature	32° F	= 0° C	
	68° F	= 20° C	
	212° F	= 100° C	

American Heart Association. *Mild Sodium Restricted Diet.* New York: American Heart Association, 1969.

American Heart Association. *Your 500 Milligram Sodium Diet.* New York: American Heart Association, 1969.

American Heart Association. *Your 1000 Milligram Sodium Diet.* New York: American Heart Association, 1968.

Bagg, Elma W. *Cooking Without a Grain of Salt.* New York: Doubleday, 1964.

Bringas, Juliet G., and Teresa Y. Chan. *1000 Milligram Sodium Diet.* Los Angeles: Nutrition in the Life Cycle, 1977.

Bringas, Juliet G., and Teresa Y. Chan. *The Sodium-Restricted Diabetic Diet.* Los Angeles: Nutrition in the Life Cycle, 1977.

Bringas, Juliet G., and Teresa Y. Chan. *Two Gram Sodium Diet.* Los Angeles: Nutrition in the Life Cycle, 1978.

Church, Helen Nichols, and Jean A. T. Pennington. *Bowes and Church's Food Values of Portions Commonly Used.* 14th rev. ed. New York: Harper & Row, 1985.

Conason, Emil G., and Ella Metz. *The Salt-Free Diet Cook Book.* New York: Grosset & Dunlap, 1969.

Johnston, Barbara, and Maria Koh. *Halt! No Salt.* Bellevue, Washington: Dietary Research, 1974.

Jones, Jeanne. *The Calculating Cook.* 2d ed., rev. San Francisco: 101 Productions, 1979.

Jones, Jeanne. *Diet for a Happy Heart.* 3d ed. San Francisco: 101 Productions, 1988.

Jones, Jeanne. *Cook It Light.* New York: Macmillan, 1987.

Jones, Jeanne. *Fabulous Fiber Cookbook.* 2d ed. San Francisco: 101 Productions, 1979.

Jones, Jeanne. *The Fabulous High-Fiber Diet.* San Francisco: 101 Productions, 1985.

Kraus, Barbara. *The Dictionary of Sodium, Fats, and Cholesterol.* New York: Grosset & Dunlap, 1977.

Leonard, Jon N., J. L. Hofer, and Nathan Pritikin. *Live Longer Now.* New York: Grosset & Dunlap, 1974.

Mayer, Jean. *A Diet for Living.* New York: Pocket Books, 1977.

Nutriplanner 6000, Practorcare (software). San Diego: Practorcare, 1987.

Payne, Alma Smith, and Dorothy Callahan. *The Fat and Sodium Control Cookbook.* Boston: Little, Brown, 1965.

Thorburn, Anna Houston, with Phyllis Turner. *Living Salt Free & Easy.* New York: Signet, 1976.

U.S. Department of Agriculture. *Composition of Foods—Raw, Processed, Prepared.* Revised Handbook 8. Washington, D.C.: Government Printing Office, 1975.

U.S. Department of Agriculture. *Nutritive Value of American Foods in Common Units.* Handbook 456. Washington, D.C.: Government Printing Office, 1975.

Albondigas, Sopa de, 27
Amaretto Peaches, 142
Amaretto Sauce, 142
Appetizers, Hors d'Oeuvres, and First Courses
   Asparagus Vinaigrette, 63
   Brussels Sprouts al Dente, 59
   Curried Orange Appetizer, 50
   Green Bean Hors d'Oeuvres, 59
   Italian Eggplant, 70
   Mushroom Hors d'Oeuvres, 64
   Seviche, 88
Apple and Cheese Salad, 52
Apple Dumplings with Brandy Sauce, 139
Applesauce Dressing, Curried, 48
Artichoke Bowls, Versatile, 62
Asian Sesame Seed Sauce, 39
Asparagus Tips, Fresh, 59
Asparagus Vinaigrette, 63

B & B Potato Boats, 74
Baked Beans, 72
Baked French Onion Soup, 24
Baked Parsley, 67
Baked Spaghetti Squash, 68
Baking Powder, Low-Sodium, 164
Banana Cream Dressing, 47
Bananas North Pole, 145
Barbecue Sauce, Lemon, 39
Barbecued Lamb, Indonesian, 113
Basic Dressing, Secret, 45
Basic Omelet, 77
Beans, Baked, 72
Béarnaise Sans Sel, Sauce, 36

Beef *See also* Veal
   Enchiladas Hamburguesas, 111
   Italian Liver, 117
   Martini Pot Roast, 109
   New England Boiled Dinner, 110
   Steak au Poivre, 108
Beef Bouillon, Unsalted, 19
Beef Consommé, Unsalted, 20
Beef Gravy, Unsalted, 30
Beef Stock, Unsalted, 16
Beverages
   Bloody Mary, 160
   Bloody Shame, 160
   Calorie Counter's Wine, 160
   Counterfeit Cocktail, 159
   Desert Tea, 162
   Fresh Fruit Frappé, 162
   High-Potassium Punch, 163
   Hot Diggity Dog, 161
   Low-Sodium Peanut Butter Punch, 163
   Piña Colada, 161
   Salty Dog, 161
   Vitality Cocktail, 159
Bloody Mary (with Vodka), 160
Bloody Shame (without Vodka), 160
Blueberry Mousse, 140
Blueberry Soup, Cold, 22
Bouillon
   Unsalted Beef, 19
   Unsalted Chicken, 19
   Unsalted Court, 18
Bread Crumbs, 119

Breads *See* also Muffins
    Blarney, 119
    Bread Crumbs, 119
    Croutons, 119
    Crunchy Low-Sodium Wheat-Berry, 122
    Dill, 126
    Lettuce, 125
    Low-Sodium French, 120
    Low-Sodium White, 121
    Low-Sodium Whole Wheat, 122
    Swedish Rye, 123
    Toasted Tortilla Triangles, 122
    Zucchini, 133
Broccoli
    Florets, 59
    Stars, 60
    Stars, Curried, 60
Browned, Onions, 63
Brown Sauce, Unsalted Light, 34
Butter, Honey, 41

Cabbage, Caraway, 70
Caesar Dressing, Secret, 44
Cakes
    Cinnamon-Lemon Cheesecake, 156
    Dieter's Dream Fruitcake, 153
    Kuchen, 144
Calorie Counter's Wine, 160
Cannelloni, Turkey, 102
Cantonese Sweet and Sour Pork, 116
Caraway Cabbage, 70
Celery Seed Dressing, 46
Cereal
    Fruity Granola, 144
    Overnight Oatmeal, 128
Cheese and Chive Omelet, 78
Cheese Salad, Apple and, 52
Cheese Salad, Pineapple and, 52

Cheesecake, Cinnamon-Lemon, 156
Chef's Salad, Vegetarian, 56
Chicken
    Bouillon, Unsalted, 19
    Consommé, Unsalted, 20
    Concord, 101
    Curaçao, 98
    Egg Foo Yung, 99
    Gravy, Unsalted, 30
    Oven-Roasted, 97
    Paella, 89
    Paprika, 100
    Salad, Rainbow, 54
    Stock, Unsalted, 17
Chinese Snow Pea and Shrimp Salad, 53
Chinese Snow Peas and Water Chestnuts, 65
Chutney, Major Jones, 40
Cinnamon-Lemon Cheesecake, 156
Cocktail Sauce, Mexican, 31
Cocktail Sauce, Unsalted, 31
Coconut Dressing, Curried, 48
Cold Blueberry Soup, 22
Cold Orange Soufflé, 146
Condiments, Commercial, about, 164
Consommé
    Unsalted Beef, 20
    Unsalted Chicken, 20
    Unsalted Madrilene, 21
    Unsalted Sherried, 20
Cornish Hens Orangeries, 96
Cottage Cheese Crêpes, 81
Cottage Cheese, Rinsing, 75
Counterfeit Cocktail, 159
Court Bouillon, Unsalted, 18
Crackers
    Low-Sodium Graham, 130
    Whole Wheat, 129

Cream Puffs, Low-Sodium, 150
Crêpes
    Low-Sodium, 134
    Cottage Cheese, 81
    Suzette, 149
Croutons, 119
Crunchy Low-Sodium Wheat-Berry Bread, 122
Cumin Dressing, Secret, 45
Curried Applesauce Dressing, 48
Curried Broccoli Stars, 60
Curried Coconut Dressing, 48
Curried Ginger Dressing, 48
Curried Orange Appetizer, 50
Curried Zucchini Purée, 66
Curry Condiment Salad, 51
Curry Dressing, Secret, 45
Curry, Indian Lamb, 115

Defatted Drippings, 29
Desert Tea, 162
Dieter's Dream Fruitcake, 153
Dill Bread, 126
Dill Sauce, Low-Sodium, 38
Dilled Onion Relish, 40
Dressings, Salad *See* Salad Dressings
Drippings, Defatted, 29

East Indian Tuna Salad, 53
Egg Dishes *See also* Omelets
    Chicken Egg Foo Yung, 99
    Cottage Cheese Crêpes, 81
Eggs Benedict, 78
    Huevos Rancheros, 82
    Lemon French Toast, 81
    Matzo Balls au Gratin, 83
    Poached Eggs, 76
    Soufflé Sans Sel, 80
Egg Substitute, 76

Eggplant
    Eggplant Sublime, 71
    Italian Eggplant, 70
Enchiladas Hamburguesas, 111
English Muffins, Low-Sodium, 124

Fast "Frozen" Yogurt, 141
Fennel Dressing, Secret, 45
Fiesta Dressing, 44
Fillet of Sole, Walnuts with, 85
Fish and Shellfish
    Fillet of Sole, Walnuts with, 85
    Fish en Papillote, 94
    Fish Fillets à la Véronique, 86
    Fish Kabobs, 93
    Paella, 89
    Pisces Mexicana, 87
    Poached Salmon, 91
    Salmon Quenelles in Dill Sauce, 92
    Seviche, 88
    Stuffed Tarragon Trout, 90
Fish Kabobs, 93
Fish Stock, Unsalted, 18
French Bread, Low-Sodium, 120
French Onion Soup, Baked, 24
French Toast, Lemon, 81
Fresh Fruit Frappé, 162
Fructose, 164
Fruit Desserts
    Amaretto Peaches, 142
    Bananas North Pole, 145
    Blueberry Mousse, 140
    Cold Orange Soufflé, 146
    Dieter's Dream Fruitcake, 153
    Fruit Frappé, Fresh, 162
    Poached Pears, 141
    Strawberries Hoffmann-La Roche, 152

Fruit Frappé, Fresh, 162
Fruitcake, Dieter's Dream, 153
Fruity Granola, 144

Gazpacho, Spicy, 22
Giant Cinnamon Popovers, 131
Giant Popovers, 131
Ginger Dressing, Curried, 48
Gingerbread Muffins, 127
Gnocchi, 136
Golden Filling, 151
Graham Crackers, Low-Sodium, 130
Granola, Fruity, 144
Gravies
    Defatted Drippings, 29
    Unsalted Beef, 30
    Unsalted Chicken, 30
    Unsalted Turkey, 30
    Green Bean Hors d'Oeuvre, 59

Hearty Lentil Soup, 23
High-Potassium Punch, 163
Hollandaise Sans Sel, Sauce, 35
Honey "Butter," 41
Hot Diggity Dog, 161
Huevos Rancheros, 82

Indian Lamb Curry, 115
Indonesian Barbecued Lamb, 113
Irish Stew, 112
Italian Dressing, Secret, 46
Italian Eggplant, 70
Italian Liver, 117

Jamaican Rice Pudding with Rum Sauce, 147
Jelled Milk, Low-Sodium, 41
Kabobs, Fish, 93
Kuchen, 144

Lamb
    Indian Lamb Curry, 115
    Indonesian Barbecued Lamb, 113
    Irish Stew, 112
    Minted Lamb Chops, 114
Lemon Barbecue Sauce, 39
Lemon French Toast, 81
Lentil Soup, Hearty, 23
Lettuce Bread, 125
Lettuce, Tarragon-Cream, 61
Light Brown Sauce, Unsalted, 34
Lithuanian Rabbit, 104
Liver, Italian, 117
Low-Cholesterol Zabaglione, 143
Low-Sodium
    Baking Powder, 164
    Cream Puffs, 150
    Crêpes, 134
    Dill Sauce, 38
    English Muffins, 124
    Jelled Milk, 41
    Matzo Balls, 137
    Pancakes, 135
    Peanut Butter Punch, 163
    Sausage, 115
    Wheat-Berry Bread, Crunchy, 122
    White Bread, 121
    Whole Wheat Bread, 122

Madrilene, Unsalted, 21
Major Jones Chutney, 40
Marinara Sauce, 32
Marinated Zucchini Spears, 65
Martini Pot Roast, 109
Matzo Balls, Low-Sodium, 137,
Matzo Balls Au Gratin, 83
Mayonnaise, Unsalted, 37

Mexican Cocktail Sauce, 31
Mexican Meatballs, 111
Milk, Low-Sodium Jelled, 41
Minestrone, 26
Minted Lamb Chops, 114
Mousse, Blueberry, 140
Muffins
    Gingerbread, 127
    Low-Sodium English, 124
    Pineapple, 128
Mushroom and, Peanut Salad, 54
Mushroom Hors d'Oeuvres, 64
Mustard Sauce, 32
Mystery Slaw, 50

New England Boiled Dinner, 110
Noodle Pudding, 148

Oat Bran Waffles, 132
Oatmeal, Overnight, 128
Omelets
    Basic, 77
    Cheese and Chive, 78
    Peaches 'n' Cream, 79
Onion-Orange Dressing, 47
Onion Relish, Dilled, 40
Onion Soup, Baked French, 24
Onions, Browned, 63
Open-Faced BLT, 68
Orange Appetizer, Curried, 50
Orange-Onion Dressing, 47
Orange Soufflé, Cold, 146
Osso Buco, 106
Oven-Roasted Chicken, 97
Oven-Roasted Turkey, 103
Overnight Oatmeal, 128

Paella, 89
Pancakes, Low-Sodium, 135

Parsley, Baked, 67
Pasta
    Gnocchi, 136
    Vegetarian Spaghetti, 69
Pea and Shrimp Salad, Chinese Snow, 53
Peas and Water Chestnuts, Chinese Snow, 65
Pea Soup, Sherried, 25
Peaches, Amaretto, 142
Peaches 'n' Cream Omelet, 79
Peanut Butter Punch, Low-Sodium, 163
Peanut Butter-Honey Pie, 154
Peanut-Mushroom Salad, 54
Pears, Poached, 141
Perfect Pumpkin Pie, 155
Perfect Salt-Free Pie Crust, 154
Pies
    Peanut Butter-Honey Pie, 154
    Perfect Pumpkin Pie, 155
Pilaf, Portuguese, 72
Piña Colada, 161
Pineapple and Cheese Salad, 52
Pineapple Muffins, 128
Pink Party Salad, 56
Pisces Mexicana, 87
Poached Eggs, 76
Poached Pears, 141
Poached Salmon, 91
Popovers, Giant, 131
Popovers, Giant Cinnamon, 131
Pork
    Cantonese Sweet and Sour Pork, 116
    Low-Sodium Sausage, 115
Portuguese Pilaf, 72
Pot Roast, Martini, 109
Potassium bicarbonate, 164
Potato Boats, B & B, 74
Potato Salad, St. Patrick's Day, 55

Poultry *See* Chicken and Rabbit
Puddings
    Jamaican Rice Pudding with Rum Sauce, 147
    Noodle Pudding, 148
Pumpkin Pie, Perfect, 155

Quenelles in Dill Sauce, Salmon, 92

Rabbit, Lithuanian, 104
Rainbow Chicken Salad, 54
Relish, Dilled Onion, 40
Rice Dishes
    Portuguese Pilaf, 72
    Wild Rice à l'Orange, 73
Rice Pudding with Rum Sauce, Jamaican, 147
Rum Sauce, 147
Rye Bread, Swedish, 123

St. Patrick's Day Potato Salad, 55
Salad Dressings
    Banana Cream, 47
    Celery Seed, 46
    Curried Applesauce, 48
    Curried Coconut, 48
    Curried Ginger, 48
    Fiesta, 44
    Orange-Onion, 47
    Secret Basic, 45
    Secret Caesar, 44
    Secret Cumin, 45
    Secret Curry, 45
    Secret Fennel, 45
    Secret Italian, 46
    Secret Tarragon, 45
    Secret Tartar Sauce, 38
    Secret Vinaigrette, 46
Salads
    Apple and Cheese, 52

Chinese Snow Pea and Shrimp, 53
Curried Orange Appetizer, 50
Curry Condiment, 51
East Indian Tuna, 53
Mystery Slaw, 50
Peanut-Mushroom, 54
Pineapple and Cheese, 52
Pink Party, 56
Rainbow Chicken, 54
St. Patrick's Day Potato, 55
Vegetarian Chef's, 56
Wilted Spanish, 51
Salmon, Poached, 91
Salmon Quenelles in Dill Sauce, 92
Sandwich
    Open-faced BLT, 68
Sauces
    Asian Sesame Seed, 39
    Béarnaise Sauce, San Sel, 36
    Brandy, 42
    Dill, Low-Sodium, 38
    Hollandaise, Sans Sel, 35
    Lemon Barbecue, 39
    Marinara, 32
    Mexican Cocktail, 31
    Mustard, 32
    Secret Tartar, 38
    Sherry-Ginger, 42
    Unsalted Cocktail, 31
    Unsalted Light Brown, 34
    Unsalted Mayonnaise, 37
    Unsalted White, 33
    Vanilla, 42
Sausage, Low-Sodium, 115
Savory Filling, 151
Savory Tomatoes Au Gratin, 67
Seafood *See* Fish and Seafood

Secret Suggestions and Important Facts, 164
Sesame Seed Sauce, Asian, 39
Seviche, 88
Sherried Consommé, Unsalted, 20
Sherried Pea Soup, 25
Shrimp Salad, Chinese Snow Pea and, 53
Smoked Turkey Breast, 104
Snow Pea and Shrimp Salad, Chinese, 53
Snow Peas and Water Chestnuts, Chinese, 65
Sopa de Albondigas, 27
Soufflé, Cold Orange, 146
Soufflé Sans Sel, 80
Soup
   Blueberry, Cold, 22
   French Onion, Baked, 24
   Gazpacho, Spicy, 22
   Lentil, Hearty, 23
   Minestrone, 26
   Sherried Pea, 25
   Sopa de Albondigas, 27
   Stracciatella alla Romana, 25
Southern Yam Casserole, 73
Spaghetti Squash, Baked, 68
Spaghetti, Vegetarian, 69
Spanish Salad, Wilted, 51
Spiced Walnuts, 143
Spicy Gazpacho, 22
Steak au Poivre, 108
Stocks
   Unsalted Beef Stock, 16
   Unsalted Beef Bouillon, 19
   Unsalted Beef Consommé, 20
   Unsalted Chicken, 17
   Unsalted Chicken Consommé, 20
   Unsalted Court Bouillon, 18
   Unsalted Fish Stock, 18
   Unsalted Madrilene, 21

Unsalted Turkey, 17
Unsalted Vegetable, 19
Stracciatella Alla Romana, 25
Strawberry Jelly, 157
Strawberries Hoffmann-La Roche, 152
Streusel Topping, 145
Stuffed Tarragon Trout, 90
Swedish Rye Bread, 123
Sweet and Sour Pork, Cantonese, 116

Tarragon-Cream Lettuce, 61
Tarragon Dressing, Secret, 45
Tarragon Trout, Stuffed, 90
Tartar Sauce, Secret, 38
Tea, Desert, 162
Toasted Tortilla Triangles, 122
Tomato Sauces
   Marinara, 32
   Mexican Cocktail, 31
   Unsalted Cocktail, 31
Tomatoes au Gratin, Savory, 67
Tortilla Triangles, Toasted, 122
Trout, Stuffed Tarragon, 90
Tuna Salad, East Indian, 53
Turkey
   Oven-Roasted Turkey, 103
   Smoked Turkey Breast, 104
Turkey Cannelloni, 102
Turkey Gravy, Unsalted, 30
Turkey Stock, Unsalted, 17
   Unsalted Beef Bouillon, 19
   Unsalted Beef Consommé, 20
   Unsalted Beef Gravy, 30
   Unsalted Beef Stock, 16
   Unsalted Chicken Bouillon, 19
   Unsalted Chicken Consommé, 20
   Unsalted Chicken Gravy, 30

Unsalted Chicken Stock, 17
Unsalted Cocktail Sauce, 31
Unsalted Court Bouillon, 18
Unsalted Fish Stock, 18
Unsalted Light Brown Sauce, 34
Unsalted Madrilene, 21
Unsalted Mayonnaise, 37
Unsalted Sherried Consommé, 20
Unsalted Turkey Gravy, 30
Unsalted Turkey Stock, 17
Unsalted Vegetable Stock, 19
Unsalted White Sauce, 33

Vanilla Sauce, 42
Veal
    Osso Buco, 106
    Veal Oscar, 107
Vegetable Dishes
    Asparagus Tips, Fresh, 59
    Asparagus Vinaigrette, 63
    B & B Potato Boats, 74
    Baked Beans, 72
    Baked Parsley, 67
    Baked Spaghetti Squash, 68
    Broccoli Florets, 59
    Broccoli Stars, 60
    Browned Onions, 63
    Brussels Sprouts al Dente, 59
    Caraway Cabbage, 70
    Chinese Snow Peas and Water Chestnuts, 65
    Curried Broccoli Stars, 60
    Curried Zucchini Purée, 66
    Dilled Onion Relish, 40
    Eggplant Sublime, 71
    Green Bean Hors d'Oeuvre, 59
    Italian Eggplant, 70
    Marinated Zucchini Spears, 65

    Mushroom Hors d'Oeuvres, 64
    Open-Faced BLT, 68
    Portuguese Pilaf, 72
    Savory Tomatoes Au Gratin, 67
    Southern Yam Casserole, 73
    Tarragon-Cream Lettuce, 61
    Vegetarian Casserole, 69
    Vegetarian Spaghetti, 69
    Versatile Artichoke Bowls, 62
    Wild Rice à l'Orange, 73
    Zucchini in Basil "Butter," 64
Vegetarian Casserole, 69
Vegetarian Chef's Salad, 56
Vegetarian Spaghetti, 69
Vinaigrette Dressing, Secret, 46
Vitality Cocktail, 159

Waffles, Oat Bran, 132
Walnuts, Spiced, 143
Water Chestnuts, Chinese Snow Peas and, 65
Wheat-Berry Bread, Crunchy Low-Sodium, 122
White Bread, Low-Sodium, 121
White Sauce, Unsalted, 33
Whole Wheat Bread, Low-Sodium, 122
Whole Wheat Crackers, 129
Wild Rice à l'Orange, 73
Wilted Spanish Salad, 51
Wine, Calorie Counter's, 160

Yam Casserole, Southern, 73
Yogurt, Fast "Frozen," 141

Zabaglione, Low-Cholesterol, 143
Zucchini Bread, 133
Zucchini in Basil "Butter," 64
Zucchini, Curried Purée, 66
Zucchini Spears, Marinated, 65

JEANNE JONES is one of the country's most popular authors, lecturers, and food columnists. Her King Feature syndicated column, "Cook It Light," reaches more than thirty million readers weekly. She also is an international spokesperson and nutritional consultant to hotels, spas, and food companies. As author of more than 20 books on light cooking, healthy eating, fitness, and well being, she has over a million copies in print. Among her best-known books are *The Calculating Cook, Diet for a Happy Heart, Cook It Light, Jeanne Jones' Food Lover's Diet, Jeanne Jones Entertains,* and *Menus & Recipes from "Cook It Light,"* the companion book to Jeanne Jones' TV cooking series.